2007
Merry Christmas,
Bradleys!!
Love,
the Herberts
XOXO

THE JOYS OF
Christmas

pil

Publications International, Ltd.

Heidi Tyline King writes about holidays, decorating, home improvement, and travel. Her work has been featured in numerous national magazines, and she has written or contributed to more than a hundred books. She and her husband live in Tallahassee, Florida, with their three daughters, who have yet to see snow.

Luci Shaw Quote
Luci Shaw, writer in residence, Regent College. Used by permission of the author.

Santa Claus Is Coming to Town
Words by HAVEN GILLESPIE, Music by J. FRED COOTS © 1934 (Renewed 1962) EMI FEIST CATALOG INC. Rights for the Extended Renewal Term in the United States Controlled by HAVEN GILLESPIE MUSIC and EMI FEIST CATALOG INC. All Rights Controlled outside the United States Controlled by EMI FEIST CATALOG INC. (Publishing) and ALFRED PUBLISHING CO., INC. (Print) All Rights Reserved

The Gift of Understanding
Excerpted from "The Gift of Understanding" by Bruce Barton. Reprinted with permission from *Reader's Digest*, December 1942. Copyright © 1942 by The Reader's Digest Assn., Inc.

Louis Weber, CEO
Publications International, Ltd.
7373 North Cicero Avenue
Lincolnwood, Illinois 60712

Permission is never granted for commercial purposes.

ISBN-13: 978-1-4127-1207-1

ISBN-10: 1-4127-1207-6

Manufactured in China.

8 7 6 5 4 3 2 1

Library of Congress Control Number: 2006902813

Contents

Catch the Spirit

Christmas spirit. It can't be bought, despite stores selling holiday decorations as early as September. No, you can't buy Christmas spirit...it must come from your heart. Adults can reminisce and recall the wonder and excitement of Christmas through the eyes of a child. At the same time, they know that love truly is the greatest of all gifts at Christmas or any time.

The Joys of Christmas is filled with inspiring quotes, poems, and heartwarming stories that will evoke your Christmas spirit. Each chapter contains familiar Christmas carols, interesting facts and trivia, and simple yet elegant holiday crafts and recipes to help you deck your halls with a festive flair.

These days, with so much emphasis placed on buying gifts, it is easy to lose sight of the real reason for the season. But "The Birth of Jesus," in Chapter 1, explains how it all began more than 2,000 years ago. This timeless story reminds us of the true meaning of Christmas.

The tender stories and poems in Chapter 2 remind us that Christmas is about spending time with family and friends and reaching out to others. Whether you're sipping cocoa by the fireplace, baking cookies, or delivering Christmas dinner to a family in need, the message is clear: Be with the ones you love.

Have you ever wondered why we send Christmas cards? Decorate an evergreen tree and give it a place of honor in our home? Smooch a sweetheart underneath a parasitic plant?

These questions and many more will be answered in Chapters 3 and 4 as *The Joys of Christmas* explores the origins of several holiday traditions.

Christmas is celebrated throughout the world, but each nation has its own unique way of commemorating this special day. Have your passport handy because in Chapter 5 we'll take a trip around the world to learn how Christmas is celebrated in various countries.

In Chapter 6, we look at the role Christmas music plays in lifting our spirits, touching our hearts, and allowing us to connect with others. As Susan Fahncke writes in "Caroling":

"True joy began to fill my soul as I sang my heart out for this man. No one had greeted us with such joy and enthusiasm all night. No one had made us feel so welcomed and so loved.... We slowly and regrettably left the man, whose spirit and tears made all the difference in our night, indeed, all the difference in our Christmas."

Did you ever wonder how Santa delivers gifts to children all over the world in just one night? Logistically speaking, it would be impossible ... but not with a little help from his friends. Children in other countries anticipate the arrival of St. Nicholas, Father Christmas, or even the Christmas gnome. In the final chapter, you'll get to know the real Santa Claus and meet his international counterparts as well.

The holiday season is a special time to get together with family and friends and to reflect upon our many blessings. It is also the perfect time to spread the Christmas spirit and to share with those in need what we are so fortunate to have. May you keep the joys of Christmas in your heart today and all year through.

CHAPTER ONE

Silent Night

Silent night! Holy night!

All is calm, all is bright,

Round yon virgin mother and Child,

Holy Infant so tender and mild;

Sleep in heavenly peace,

Sleep in heavenly peace.

—JOSEPH MOHR

Joseph Mohr, a curate in an Alpine village in Austria, first wrote *"Stille Nacht"* as a poem in 1816. On Christmas Eve two years later, Mohr, who had become the new assistant pastor at St. Nicholas Church in Oberndorf, asked organist Franz Gruber to help set his poem to music. Working all day on the song, the two sang "Silent Night" for the congregation that night at mass.

Years later, Karl Mauracher, an organ builder who was visiting the church, found the song and passed it along to the Rainer and Strasser families, folksingers who performed throughout Europe and even as far as the United States. For the next 20 years, the families included the song in their repertoires. The more "Silent Night" was played, the more the song grew in popularity. Today, almost 200 years later, "Silent Night" has been translated into 300 languages and is regarded as the world's most widely sung Christmas carol.

Love came down at Christmas;

Love all lovely, Love Divine;

Love was born at Christmas,

Stars and angels gave the sign.

—Christina Rossetti

Let us keep Christmas beautiful without a thought of greed,
That it might live forevermore to fill our every need,
That it shall not be just a day, but last a lifetime through,
The miracle of Christmastime that brings God close to you.

—ANN SCHULTZ

The First Christmas

Long ago in Nazareth, the angel Gabriel appeared to a young woman named Mary, who was engaged to Joseph, a carpenter. The angel told Mary, "Rejoice! The Lord is with you. Do not be afraid, Mary. God has greatly blessed you. You are going to have a baby, and you will name him Jesus. He will be the Son of God. His kingdom will never end."

Joseph was worried about Mary having a baby that was not his, but Gabriel appeared to him in a dream, so that he would understand about the Holy Child and wed Mary.

Some months later, the couple set out for Bethlehem to pay their taxes. Mary was nearing the time when she would give birth, which made the trip particularly difficult for her. Even worse, when they arrived, there was

no room at any of the inns. One innkeeper noticed that Mary was heavy with child and offered to let the couple stay in his stable.

That night, Mary gave birth to her baby, the Son of God. She wrapped the babe in swaddling cloths and laid him in a manger. Mary and Joseph named the baby Jesus.

Outside in the night sky, a bright new star appeared in the east. This was a very special star and it shone like no other. It has come to be known as the Star of Bethlehem.

In the fields outside the town, shepherds were keeping watch over their sheep throughout the night. Suddenly there was a great light, and an angel of the Lord appeared before them. The shepherds were very frightened.

The angel spoke to the shepherds, saying, "Fear not, for I bring you wonderful news. It will bring great joy to all the world. For there is born to you this night in Bethlehem a Savior, who is Christ the Lord. And this is how you will know him: You will find a baby wrapped in swaddling cloths, lying in a manger."

Then all at once many angels appeared in the sky. The angels sang praises:

"Glory to God in the highest, and on earth peace and goodwill toward all people." The shepherds said to one another, "Let us go to this baby that God's angels have told us about."

The shepherds hurried to Bethlehem through the bright, starlit night. Soon they found Mary and Joseph resting in the stable and the Baby Jesus wrapped in swaddling cloths asleep in the manger.

Three wise men also saw the star and knew it was a sign that the Savior had been born. They learned that Bethlehem was the birthplace, so they decided to go worship the newborn King. They gathered gifts of gold, frankincense, and myrrh, and set off on their long journey.

The Three Wise Men traveled the long road to Bethlehem with their gifts for the Baby Jesus. To their great joy and wonder, the same bright star that they had seen first in the east went ahead of them. Its light guided them on their long journey. The star's ever-present glow led them over the hills and across valleys.

The Wise Men followed the star westward until they reached Bethlehem. Then the star seemed to stand still, beaming light down on a small stable. The Wise Men knew that this must be where Baby Jesus lay.

Inside the stable, they saw the baby with his mother, Mary. Gazing on the child, the Wise Men fell to their knees and worshipped the infant. They opened the treasures they had brought from the East and presented the infant Jesus with the rare gifts of gold, frankincense, and myrrh.

Soon others came from across the land to worship the newborn Son of God. To this day, people from all over the world celebrate Christmas to commemorate Jesus' birth.

— SARAH TOAST

We Three Kings

JOHN HENRY HOPKINS, JR.

We three kings of Orient are,
Bearing gifts we traverse afar,
Field and fountain, moor and
   mountain,
Following yonder star.

O—star of wonder, star of night,
Star with royal beauty bright,
Westward leading, still proceeding,
Guide us to thy perfect light.

Born a King on Bethlehem's plain,
Gold I bring to crown him again,
King forever, ceasing never,
Over us all to reign.

Frankincense to offer have I,
Incense owns a deity nigh.
Prayer and praising, all men raising,
Worship him, God most high.

Myrrh is mine, its bitter perfume,
Breathes a life of gathering gloom;
Sorrowing, sighing, bleeding, dying,
Sealed in the stone-cold tomb.

Glorious now behold him arise,
King and God and sacrifice,
Alleluia, Alleluia;
Earth to the heav'ns replies.

Gold

The gift of gold to the Christ Child is supposed to have come from Melchior, a king from Arabia, who, legend has it, was one of the Three Wise Men. His contribution is thought to have financed the Holy Family's flight into Egypt. Gold, as valuable today as it was in Christ's time, symbolizes immortality, divinity, purity, and the kingship of Jesus Christ.

What babe new born is this that in a manger cries?
Near on her lowly bed his happy mother lies.
Oh, see the air is shaken with white and heavenly wings—
This is the Lord of all the earth, this is the King of Kings.

—RICHARD WATSON GILDER, *A CHRISTMAS HYMN*

The Birth of Jesus

In those days Caesar Augustus issued a decree that a census should be taken of the entire Roman world. (This was the first census that took place while Quirinius was governor of Syria.) And everyone went to his own town to register.

So Joseph also went up from the town of Nazareth in Galilee to Judea, to Bethlehem the town of David, because he belonged to the house and line of David. He went there to register with Mary, who was pledged to be married to him and was expecting a child. While they were there, the time came for the baby to be born, and she gave birth to her firstborn, a son. She wrapped him in cloths and placed him in a manger, because there was no room for them in the inn.

And there were shepherds living out in the fields nearby, keeping watch over their flocks at night. An angel of the Lord appeared to them, and the glory of the Lord shone around them, and they were terrified. But the angel said to them, "Do not be afraid. I bring you good news of great joy that will be for all the people. Today in the town of David a Savior has been born to you; he is Christ the Lord. This will be a sign to you: You will find a baby wrapped in cloths and lying in a manger."

Suddenly a great company of the heavenly host appeared with the angel, praising God and saying, "Glory to God in the highest, and on earth peace to men on whom his favor rests."

When the angels had left them and gone into heaven, the shepherds

said to one another, "Let's go to Bethlehem and see this thing that has happened, which the Lord has told us about."

So they hurried off and found Mary and Joseph, and the baby, who was lying in the manger. When they had seen him, they spread the word concerning what had been told them about this child, and all who heard it were amazed at what the shepherds said to them. But Mary treasured up all these things and pondered them in her heart. The shepherds returned, glorifying and praising God for all the things they had heard and seen, which were just as they had been told.

—LUKE 2:1–20, NIV

Bethlehem of Judea

A little child,
A shining star.
A stable rude,
The door ajar.

Yet in that place,
So crude, forlorn,
The Hope of all
The world was born.

—AUTHOR UNKNOWN

Frankincense

Tradition maintains that Balthasar, one of the Three Wise Men who came from the East to find the Christ Child, presented frankincense to the baby as a gift. By honoring him in this way, Balthasar fulfilled the prophecy that gold and frankincense would be brought

from the Gentiles to honor the heavenly king (Isaiah 60 and Psalm 72).

Frankincense, a sweet gum resin from the Boswellia tree, is the purest of incense. When burned, it produces white smoke and a sweet smell, symbolizing the prayers and praises of the faithful as well as Christ's sacrifice and the divine name of God.

The Advent Wreath

The season of Advent is the beginning of the church year for Christians. It starts the fourth Sunday before Christmas Day and ends on Christmas Eve. Meaning "arrival," Advent is a celebration of the birth of Jesus and his eventual return.

Many families celebrate this holy season by lighting an Advent wreath. A circular evergreen wreath is laid flat and adorned with four candles around the wreath and one in the center. It is very symbolic.

- The circular shape of the wreath epitomizes God himself, his endless mercy, and eternity, which has no beginning or end.
- The green pine boughs signify hope in God and eternal life.
- Candles reflect the light of Jesus coming into the world.

The four purple candles around the wreath stand for the four Sundays of Advent and for the four centuries between the time the prophet Malachi predicted the coming of the Messiah and the actual birth of Jesus. One purple candle is lit for each Sunday in Advent, with one candle lit on the first Sunday, two on the second Sunday, and so on, until all four candles are lit on the fourth Sunday. The white center candle symbolizes Christmas Day and is lit on that day.

First Live Nativity Scene

In a cave on a windswept Italian mountainside, Francis of Assisi assembled the first Christmas crib in 1223. The Christ Child, placed on an altar of stone, and two live animals—an ox and a donkey—were its only occupants. Today, a tiny monastery surrounds the cave, which still remains relatively undisturbed by the years. The idea behind the crib was to make the story of Christ's birth more vivid in the minds of shepherds and farmers who lived there. The townspeople were very enthusiastic...they were the ones who suggested the ox and donkey.

—MARK LINK

Myrrh

Caspar, a king from Tarsus and one of the Three Wise Men, is believed to have given myrrh to the Baby Jesus. Myrrh is known for its medicinal value and was used in ancient times for cleaning wounds and sores, as an analgesic, and for embalming the dead or anointing kings.

Myrrh is actually an aromatic gum resin that oozes from gashes cut in the bark of the commiphora tree. It hardens into teardrop-shaped chunks and is then pounded into powder or mixed to make ointments and perfumes. It is named for its bitter taste and symbolizes the Suffering Savior, the Great Physician, and Christ's human nature.

*Go tell it
on the
mountain,*
Over the hills and
ev'rywhere,
Go tell it on the
mountain,
That Jesus Christ is
born!

—ANONYMOUS,
AMERICAN FOLK HYMN

The Twelve Days of Christmas

One of the holiday's best-loved songs, "The Twelve Days of Christmas," marks the longest holiday in the Christian calendar—the time between Christmas Day and Epiphany, celebrated on January 6. The song's origin is unknown, but some believe the song was written to help Catholic children remember various articles of faith. These are:

True love	God
A partridge in a pear tree	Jesus
Two turtle doves	Old and New Testaments
Three French hens	Faith, Hope, and Charity
Four calling birds	Four Gospels
Five golden rings	The first five books of the Old Testament, the Pentateuch, which records the history and laws of ancient Israel
Six geese a-laying	Six days of Creation
Seven swans a-swimming	Seven gifts of the Holy Spirit, or the Seven Sacraments
Eight maids a-milking	Eight beatitudes
Nine ladies dancing	Nine fruits of the Holy Spirit
Ten lords a-leaping	Ten Commandments
Eleven pipers piping	Eleven faithful disciples
Twelve drummers drumming	Twelve points of doctrine in the Apostles' Creed

With more than 450 figures and hundreds of yards of landscape, the *world's largest diorama of the Nativity* is found in *Einsiedeln, Switzerland.* In the 1930s, crib maker Ferdinand Pottmesser built a giant Christmas crib along with hundreds of figurines. Pottmesser sold the collection to Einsiedeln in the mid-1950s, and the figurines became the impetus for creating a giant diorama—a copy of the landscape of Bethlehem and a visually accurate representation of the story of the birth of Christ. The diorama starts with angels awakening the shepherds with news of the birth of Jesus and ends with Joseph and Mary fleeing into Egypt to escape Herod and his soldiers. The diorama attracts thousands of visitors every year.

The Friendly Beasts

Author Unknown

Jesus, our brother, strong and good,
Was humbly born in a stable rude;
And the friendly beasts around him
   stood,
Jesus, our brother, strong and good.

"I," said the donkey, shaggy and
   brown.
"I carried his mother uphill and down;
I carried her safely to Bethlehem
   town,
I," said the donkey, shaggy and brown.

"I," said the cow, all white and red.
"I gave him my manger for his bed;
I gave him my hay to pillow his head;
I," said the cow, all white and red.

"I," said the sheep, with curly horn,
"I gave him my wool for his blanket
   warm,
He wore my coat on Christmas morn,
I," said the sheep, with curly horn.

"I," said the dove from rafters high.
"Cooed him to sleep so he would
   not cry,
We cooed him to sleep, my mate
   and I;
I," said the dove from rafters high.

And every beast, by some good spell,
In the stable dark was glad to tell,
Of the gift he gave Emmanuel,
The gift he gave Emmanuel.

"*Christmas began in the heart of God.* It is complete only when it reaches the heart of man."

—AUTHOR UNKNOWN

Our house is open,
  Lord, to thee;
Come in, and share
  our Christmas tree!
We've made each nook
  and corner bright,
Burnished with yellow
  candle-light.

But light that never
  burns away
Is only thine, Lord
  Jesus, stay,
Shine on us now, our
  Christmas Cheer—
Fill with thy flame our
  whole New Year!

—LUCI SHAW

"Away in a Manger" is a sweet song often sung by caroling children. It was originally published in a Lutheran Sunday school book in 1885 in Philadelphia, Pennsylvania. Two years later, James R. Murray published it as "Luther's Cradle Hymn," which set off a never-ending controversy about its origin. Because of the title, some people think Martin Luther himself wrote the words, but the song is virtually unknown in Germany—and it bears no resemblance to Luther's musical style. Others credit Murray with penning the lyrics. Generally, the words to the song are considered anonymous but American in origin. The music's history is just as elusive. It is thought that Murray either wrote the tune or was inspired by an old German folk song.

Away in a Manger

AUTHOR UNKNOWN

Away in a manger, no crib for a bed,
The little Lord Jesus laid down his sweet head.
The stars in the sky looked down where he lay,
The little Lord Jesus asleep on the hay.

The cattle are lowing, the poor baby wakes,
But little Lord Jesus, no crying he makes.
I love thee, Lord Jesus, look down from the sky,
And stay by my cradle 'til morning is nigh.

Be near me, Lord Jesus, I ask thee to stay,
Close by me forever, and love me, I pray.
Bless all the dear children in thy tender care,
And fit us for heaven, to live with thee there.

So remember while
December

Brings the only
Christmas Day,

In the year let there be
Christmas

In the things you do
and say;

Wouldn't life be worth
the living

Wouldn't dreams be
coming true

*If we kept the
Christmas
spirit*

All the whole year
through?

—AUTHOR UNKNOWN

Did You Know?

Some people think of *Xmas* as a contemporary, sacrilegious abbreviation of the word *Christmas*. On the contrary, the first letter of the word *Christ* in the Greek language is *chi*, which is identical to the modern Roman alphabet's *X*. Therefore, *Xmas* is an ecclesiastical abbreviation that has been used for almost as long as Christmas has been in existence.

The Birthplace of Jesus

It was prophesied in Micah 5:2 that Bethlehem would be the birthplace of the future King of the Jews. Indeed, this small Judean city near Jerusalem became the site of the Nativity. Bethlehem, which means "house of bread," was also the home of David, one of God's favorite kings.

Though the exact location of Jesus' birth is unknown, the story maintains that Jesus was born in a stable and laid in a manger, or food trough. In those days, stables were made of stones or situated in a cave. Around A.D. 326–330, Empress Helena, wife of Constantine, built a church over the cave thought to be Jesus' birthplace. The church was rebuilt in the sixth century, and pieces of the original building still remain. It is said to be the oldest Christian church in existence and one of the most genuinely holy sites in the Holy Land.

This altar inside the Church of the Nativity in Bethlehem is believed to mark the exact place of Jesus' birth.

Christmas in Bethlehem. The ancient dream: a cold, clear night made brilliant by a glorious star, the smell of incense, shepherds and wise men falling to their knees in adoration of the sweet baby, the incarnation of perfect love.

—LUCINDA FRANKS

O Little Town of Bethlehem

PHILLIPS BROOKS

O little town of Bethlehem,
How still we see thee lie;
Above thy deep and dreamless sleep
The silent stars go by.
Yet in thy dark streets shineth,
The everlasting light;
The hopes and fears of all the years,
Are met in thee tonight.

For Christ is born of Mary,
And gathered all above,
While mortals sleep, the angels keep
Their watch of wond'ring love.
O morning stars, together,
Proclaim the holy birth,
And praises sing to God the King,
And peace to men on earth!

How silently, how silently,
The wondrous gift is giv'n!
So God imparts to human hearts
The blessings of his heav'n.
No ear may hear his coming,
But in this world of sin,
Where meek souls will receive
    him still,
The dear Christ enters in.

O Holy Child of Bethlehem,
Descend to us, we pray;
Cast out our sin and enter in;
Be born in us today!
We hear the Christmas angels
The great glad tidings tell;
O come to us, abide with us,
Our Lord Emmanuel!

CHAPTER TWO

Over the River and Through the Woods

Over the river and through the woods

To Grandfather's house we go.

The horse knows the way to carry the sleigh

Through the white and drifted snow.

—LYDIA MARIA CHILD

An ode to grandparents everywhere, *"Over the River and Through the Woods"* was written by Lydia Maria Child about winter holidays in New England. The poem first appeared in *Flowers for Children, Vol. 2,* in 1844, but after being set to music, it became a beloved Christmas favorite throughout the United States.

Lydia Child was one of the first American women to make a living as a writer, and her repertoire included a popular domestic advice book called *The Frugal Housewife,* an early American magazine for children known as *Juvenile Miscellany,* antislavery writings, novels, and newspaper articles. During her lifetime, she was best known for her books, but as time has passed she is now remembered for her holiday song.

At Christmas the Heart Goes Home

At Christmas all roads lead home. The filled planes, packed trains, overflowing buses, all speak eloquently of a single destination: home. Despite the crowding and the crushing, the delays, the confusion, we clutch our bright packages and beam our anticipation. We are like birds driven by an instinct we only faintly understand—the hunger to be with our own people.

—Marjorie Holmes, *At Christmas the Heart Goes Home*

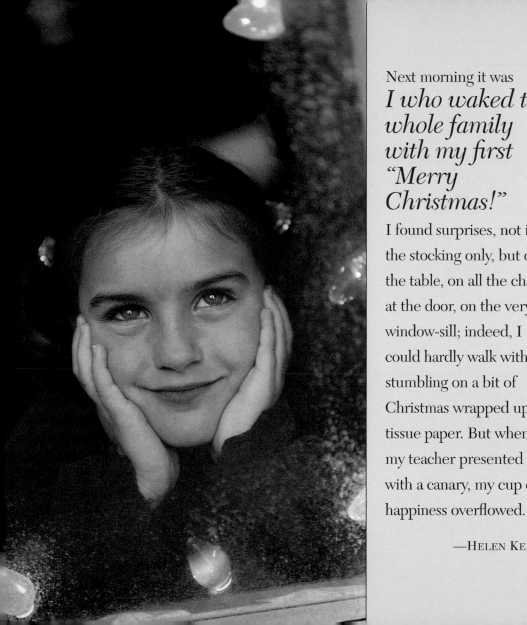

Next morning it was *I who waked the whole family with my first "Merry Christmas!"* I found surprises, not in the stocking only, but on the table, on all the chairs, at the door, on the very window-sill; indeed, I could hardly walk without stumbling on a bit of Christmas wrapped up in tissue paper. But when my teacher presented me with a canary, my cup of happiness overflowed.

—HELEN KELLER

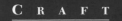

Holiday Photo Cards

Looking back at all those old Christmas photo cards brings back memories of happy holidays and those beautiful faces that make the yuletide so much fun. Now you can make your own greeting card and attach the picture yourself. With a rubber stamp and stamp pad, and embossing powder and heat gun, your card will be the hit of the season!

WHAT YOU'LL NEED

10×7-inch piece blue art paper
Waxed paper
Snowflake rubber stamp
Silver pigment ink pad
Silver embossing powder
Embossing heat gun
Extra-fine silver paint marker
4 black photo corners
3½×5-inch photograph

1 Fold blue paper in half to form 5×7-inch card. Place card on sheet of waxed paper.

2 Apply silver ink to rubber stamp by brushing ink pad against surface of stamp.

3 Starting in a corner and working quickly but carefully, firmly press inked stamp to edge of card. Repeat around entire edge of card, turning stamp in different directions, to form a border of silver snowflakes. Re-ink stamp as necessary.

4 While ink is still wet, completely cover all stamped areas with embossing powder. Shake off excess powder and return to bottle.

5 Using embossing gun, heat snowflakes until powder melts and a shiny, raised surface forms.

6 Use paint marker to write a holiday greeting inside of card.

7 Put photo corners on each corner of photograph. Moisten backs of photo corners and center photo on front of card, pressing down firmly on each corner.

Selfishness makes
Christmas a burden;
love makes it a
delight.

—Anonymous

A Kid's Guide to Christmas Around the Clock

12:30 A.M. Toss and turn in bed, anticipating Santa's arrival, before nodding off to dreams of sugarplums.

3:00 A.M. Awake to a bump in the night; tiptoe downstairs—Santa hasn't arrived.

3:45 A.M. Back to sleep after trying to stay up to see Santa.

6:00 A.M. Downstairs again to discover that, yes, Santa has come! Check out stocking stuffers and run back upstairs to wake Brother and Sister, Mom and Dad.

7:00 A.M. Stockings emptied and presents opened. Paper is everywhere.

10:00 A.M. A quick breakfast at the table with family before rushing back to toys.

12:30 P.M. On Mom's orders, take a shower and get dressed in holiday duds.

1:00 P.M. Family starts arriving; show everyone presents and decorations.

2:30 P.M. Outside to throw the football and build snowmen.

3:00 P.M. Inside for hot chocolate and a piece of Aunt Edna's carrot cake.

4:30 P.M. Play with toys with cousins.

6:00 P.M. Dinner with family: aunts and uncles, cousins, grandparents, Mom, Dad, and siblings.

7:30 P.M. Help clear the table; settle on floor in living room to play with presents and watch Christmas specials on television.

9:00 P.M. Kiss everyone good-bye; go upstairs to put on pajamas.

9:30 P.M. Insist on staying up to play with toys.

10:00 P.M. Accidentally fall asleep on the floor, with toys scattered all around.

Easy Cocoa Mix

2 cups nonfat dry milk powder

1 cup sugar

¾ cup powdered nondairy creamer

½ cup unsweetened cocoa powder

¼ teaspoon salt

1. Combine all ingredients in medium bowl until well blended. Spoon into 1-quart airtight food storage jar with tight-fitting lid.

2. Seal jar. Cover top of jar with 8-inch circle of fabric, if desired; attach serving instructions on gift tag with raffia or ribbon. *Makes about 4 cups mix or 16 servings*

FOR SINGLE SERVING: Place ¼ cup Easy Cocoa Mix in mug or cup; add ¾ cup boiling water. Stir until mix is dissolved. Top with sweetened whipped cream and marshmallows, if desired. Serve immediately.

COCOA MARSHMALLOW MIX: Prepare Easy Cocoa Mix as directed in 2-quart airtight container, adding 1 package (10½ ounces) miniature marshmallows.

FOR SINGLE SERVING: Place ½ cup Cocoa Marshmallow Mix in mug or cup; add ¾ cup boiling water. Stir until mix is dissolved. Serve immediately.

Spiced-Up Cocoa Mix

1 cup granulated sugar
½ cup unsweetened cocoa powder
1 tablespoon all-purpose flour
2 teaspoons ground cinnamon
1½ teaspoons ground cloves
½ teaspoon salt
½ teaspoon chili powder
¼ teaspoon ground allspice
½ cup (about 30) miniature marshmallows

Whisk together all ingredients except marshmallows in small mixing bowl. Place mixture in 1-pint jar with tight-fitting lid. Place marshmallows in resealable food storage bag; place bag in jar. (Add or remove marshmallows as space allows.) Cover top of jar with fabric; attach serving instructions on gift tag with raffia or ribbon.   *Makes one 1-pint jar*

GIFT TAG: Boil ⅓ cup water in 2-quart saucepan. Whisk in ¾ cup cocoa mix, stirring constantly. Continue stirring over low heat 1 to 2 minutes or until thick and smooth. Remove pan from heat; add 4 cups milk and ¾ teaspoon vanilla. Heat to steaming over medium heat, stirring constantly. Pour cocoa into 4 mugs and top with marshmallows.   *Makes 4 servings*

The Christmas Angels

It was December 23, 1993. For a single mom who was going to college and supporting my children completely alone, Christmas was looking bleak. I looked around my little home, realization dawning like a slow, twisting pain. We were poor.

Our tiny house had two bedrooms, both off the living room. They were so small that my baby daughter's crib barely fit into one room, and my son's twin bed and dresser were squeezed into the other. There was no way they could share a room, so I made my bed every night on the living room floor. The three of us shared the only closet in the house. We were snug, always only a few feet from each other, day and night. With no doors on the children's rooms, I could see and hear them at all times. It made them feel secure, and it made me feel close to them—a blessing I wouldn't have had in other circumstances.

It was early evening, about eight o'clock. The snow was falling softly, silently, and my children were both asleep. I was wrapped in a blanket, sitting at the window, watching the powdery flakes flutter in the dimming light, when my front door vibrated with a pounding fist.

Alarmed, I wondered who would stop by unannounced on such a snowy winter night. I opened the door to find a group of strangers grinning from ear to ear, their arms laden with boxes and bags.

Confused, but finding their joyous spirit contagious, I grinned right back at them.

"Are you Susan?" The man stepped forward as he held out a box for me.

Nodding stupidly, unable to find my voice, I was sure they thought I was mentally deficient.

"These are for you." The woman thrust another box at me with a huge, beaming smile. The porch light and the snow falling behind her cast a glow over her dark hair, lending her an angelic appearance.

I looked down into her box. It was filled to the top with delicious treats, a fat turkey, and all the makings of a traditional Christmas dinner. My eyes filled with tears as the realization of why they were there washed over me.

Finally coming to my senses, I found my voice and invited them in. Following the husband were two children, staggering with the weight of their packages. The family introduced themselves and told me their packages were all gifts for my little family. This wonderful, beautiful family, who were total strangers to me, somehow knew exactly what we needed. They brought wrapped gifts for each of us, a full buffet for me to make on Christmas Day, and many "extras" that I could never afford. Visions of a beautiful, "normal" Christmas literally danced in my

head. Somehow my secret wish for Christmas was materializing right in front of me. The desperate prayers of a single mom had been heard, and I knew right then that God had sent his angels my way.

My mysterious angels then handed me a white envelope, gave me another round of grins, and took turns hugging me. They wished me a Merry Christmas and disappeared into the night as suddenly as they had appeared.

Amazed and deeply touched, I looked around me at the boxes and gifts strewn at my feet and felt the ache of depression suddenly being transformed into a childlike joy. I began to cry. I cried hard, sobbing tears of the deepest gratitude. A great sense of peace filled me. The knowledge of God's love reaching into my tiny corner of the world enveloped me like a warm quilt. My heart was full. I fell to my knees amid all the boxes and offered a heartfelt prayer of thanks.

Getting to my feet, I wrapped myself in my blankets and sat once again to gaze out the window at the gently falling snow. Suddenly, I remembered the envelope. Like a child, I ripped it open and gasped at what I saw. A shower of bills flitted to the floor. Gathering them up, I began to count the five, ten, and twenty-dollar bills. As my vision blurred with tears, I counted the money, then recounted it to make sure I had it right. Sobbing again, I said it out loud: "One hundred dollars."

I looked at my children sleeping soundly, and through my tears I smiled my first happy, free-of-worry smile in a long, long time. My smile turned into a grin as I thought about tomorrow: Christmas Eve. One visit from complete strangers had magically turned a painful day into a special one that we would always remember...with happiness.

It is now several years since our Christmas angels visited. I have remarried, and our household is happy and richly blessed. Every year since that Christmas in 1993, we have chosen a family less blessed than we are. We bring them carefully selected gifts, food and treats, and as much money as we can spare. It's our way of passing on what was given to us. It's the "ripple effect" in motion. We hope that the cycle continues and that, someday, the families we share with will be able to pass it on, too.

—SUSAN FAHNCKE

Somehow not only for Christmas,
But all the long year through,
The joy that you give to others
Is the joy that comes back to you.
And the more you spend blessing
The poor and lonely and sad,
The more of your heart's possessing
Returns to make you glad.

—JOHN GREENLEAF WHITTIER,
    "THE JOY OF GIVING"

Cinnamon Sugared Pumpkin-Pecan Muffins

8 tablespoons sugar, divided

2½ to 3 teaspoons ground cinnamon, divided

1 cup 100% bran cereal

1 cup fat-free (skim) milk

1 cup all-purpose flour

1 tablespoon baking powder

½ teaspoon baking soda

½ teaspoon salt

1 cup solid-pack pumpkin

1 egg, beaten

1 tablespoon vanilla

1 package (2 ounces) pecan chips (½ cup)

1. Preheat oven to 400°F. Spray 12 (2½-inch) muffin pan cups with nonstick cooking spray; set aside. Combine 2 tablespoons sugar and ½ to 1 teaspoon cinnamon in small bowl for topping; set aside.

2. Blend cereal and milk in large bowl; set aside 5 minutes to soften. Meanwhile, combine flour, remaining 6 tablespoons sugar, remaining cinnamon, baking powder, baking soda, and salt in large bowl; mix well.

3. Whisk pumpkin, egg, and vanilla into cereal mixture. Gently fold in flour mixture just until blended. *Do not overmix.* Spoon equal amounts of batter into prepared muffin cups; sprinkle evenly with pecan chips. Sprinkle with cinnamon-sugar topping.

4. Bake 20 to 25 minutes or until toothpick inserted into centers comes out clean. Cool on wire rack 3 minutes before removing muffins from pan. Serve warm or at room temperature.   *Makes 12 servings*

festive facts

1. The average American family spends about $800 on Christmas gifts every year.

2. Thirty-seven million fresh Christmas trees are sold each year.

3. Alabama was the first state to recognize Christmas as an official holiday, starting in 1836.

4. More than 1.76 billion candy canes are made annually for the Christmas season.

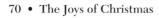

As the youngest of six children from a very close family, *I always enjoy going home for the holidays* to spend time with my mother and siblings. Hanging out in the warmth and familiarity of my mother's kitchen brings back fond memories. We all sit around the table eating and telling stories, basically all talking at once and therefore making a lot of noise. It sometimes gets so loud that I get a headache before the end of the night. However, it is one of those comforting aches, much like the sore muscles I have after a really good workout.

—BONNIE BLAIR, *HOME FOR THE HOLIDAYS*

Classic Holiday Movies

Miracle on 34th Street

It's a Wonderful Life

Holiday Inn

White Christmas

The Lemon Drop Kid

Rudolph the Red-Nosed Reindeer

The Santa Clause

And that, of course, is the message of Christmas.

We are never alone.

—Taylor Caldwell

*Christmas isn't just a day,
it's a frame of mind.*

KRIS KRINGLE, *MIRACLE ON 34TH STREET*

Lost Mitten Tree Folk Art Pillow

Creating a warm atmosphere at Christmastime is one of the pleasures of the season. You don't need a fireplace to create that warmth; homemade decorations can do the trick. This folk art pillow is sure to be one of your family's favorites!

WHAT YOU'LL NEED

Felt: 3 shades of green, 6×9 inches each; gold, 5-inch square; scraps of red, orange, purple, pink, turquoise, about 2×3 inches each

Scissors

Iron-on adhesive

Iron, ironing board

White paper

Pencil

2 square, red-fringed napkins, 18 inches each

Straight pins

Thread to match napkins

Sewing machine

8-ounce bag fiberfill

Toothpicks

Washable glue

1 Cut pieces of iron-on adhesive to match sizes of felt pieces and, following manufacturer's directions, adhere to felt.

2 Trace mitten and star patterns onto white paper and cut out. On paper backing of a shade of green felt, trace 4 mittens. Turn pattern over and trace 4 more times. On both other colors of green felt, trace 3 mittens in each direction. (You will have a total of 20 mittens.) Trace a star on paper backing of gold felt.

3 From gold and remaining colors of felt, cut small hearts, stars, circles, squares, V-shapes, zigzag lines, straight lines, and wavy lines. These will be used to decorate the mittens.

4 Arrange undecorated mittens on napkin in a pyramid shape with 6 mittens on the bottom (leave room at top for star). Each row should have one less mitten than the row below it. Make a chart of how you have your mittens arranged. Remove all but bottom row of mittens from napkin.

5 Select some colorful felt shapes to embellish your bottom row of mittens. Trim them to fit mittens. Remove paper backing from embellishments and mittens. Following manufacturer's directions, fuse embellishments and mittens to napkin. (Fusing may take several seconds longer than suggested, due to thickness of felt.)

6 Referring to your chart, replace next row of 5 mittens, removing paper backings and embellishing them as you go. Fuse to napkin. Repeat for each remaining row of mittens. Adhere gold star to top of mitten tree.

7 Matching edges, pin 2 napkins with wrong sides together. Machine stitch about ⅛ inch inside fringe around pillow, leaving about 8 inches open on bottom.

8 Stuff pillow with entire bag of fiberfill. Sew bottom opening closed.

9 If some felt pieces have not adhered well, use a toothpick to spread washable glue underneath both sides.

Enlarge patterns 150%.

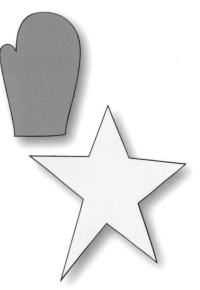

There's more, much more to Christmas
Than candlelight and cheer;
It's the spirit of sweet friendship
That brightens all the year;
It's thoughtfulness and kindness,
It's hope reborn again,
For peace, for understanding
And for goodwill to men!

—ANONYMOUS

Born on Christmas Day

1642 Sir Isaac Newton, scientist

1821 Clara Barton, nurse, founder of the American Red Cross

1878 Louis Chevrolet, co-founder of Chevrolet

1887 Conrad Hilton, hotelier

1899 Humphrey Bogart, actor

1907 Cab Calloway, jazz musician

1924 Rod Serling, writer

1946 Jimmy Buffett, musician

1949 Sissy Spacek, actor

1954 Annie Lennox, singer

1958 Rickey Henderson, baseball player

Side by side

Or miles apart

Christmas binds us

Heart to heart.

—ANONYMOUS

There's a ribbon 'round this spinning world
That binds us like a tether,
It's woven of our true beliefs
And ties us all together.

Gift-wrapped, we stand a nation true,
And bound by pride and love,
For as we dance amid the stars,
We're cradled from above.

This Christmas, let us say once more:
We pledge to love our brother,
And let us live each day as though
We care about each other.

When all days become Christmas,
And strife is nevermore,
We'll thrive, a true community,
Forever free of war.

—GAIL DODGE

May you have the gladness of Christmas which is hope;

The spirit of Christmas which is peace;

The heart of Christmas which is love.

—Ada V. Hendricks

CHAPTER THREE

We Wish You a Merry Christmas

We wish you a Merry Christmas;

We wish you a Merry Christmas;

We wish you a Merry Christmas

And a Happy New Year.

Good tidings we bring

To you and your kin;

Good tidings for Christmas

And a Happy New Year!

—AUTHOR UNKNOWN

In the 16th century, watchmen, or "waits," would blow an oboelike instrument from the town tower to signal the time to the whole village. Waits eventually evolved into groups of traveling musicians who played at official occasions, including Christmas. It is thought that the song *"We Wish You a Merry Christmas"* originated from these performers. In those days, singing carols like this one was the most blessed, joyful way to pass along Christmas greetings.

The Origin of Gift Giving

The first gifts given at Christmas were from the Magi (Wise Men) to Baby Jesus. Later, in Roman times, gift giving was popular during Saturnalia, a winter solstice celebration. The tradition as we know it today is derived from St. Nicholas, a bishop who was known for giving children presents. His long flowing red and white bishop's robes were the inspiration for Santa's modern-day costume. St. Nicholas Day, celebrated on December 6, marks a day for gift giving throughout Europe.

Did You Know...

- You can spend your holidays in these destinations: Christmas, Florida; Santa Claus, Indiana; Noel, Missouri; and Rudolph, Wisconsin.

- The Salvation Army collection kettle evolved from a large stewing pot set out in the streets of San Francisco in 1891 to collect money to provide Christmas dinner to 1,000 of the city's poorest residents.

- In the United States, many retailers make up to 70 percent of their annual revenues in the month preceding Christmas.

- More diamonds are purchased during the Christmas season than at any other time of the year.

Christmas gift suggestions:

To your enemy, forgiveness. To an opponent, tolerance. To a friend, your heart. To a customer, service. To all, charity. To every child, a good example. To yourself, respect.

—OREN ARNOLD

*Gifts of time
and love are
surely the basic
ingredients of a
truly merry
Christmas.*

—PEG BRACKEN

Classic Holiday Toys

Can't decide what to get the little tyke? Check out this list of America's favorite toys over the years, compiled by the Toy Industry Association.

Toy	Year Introduced
Parcheesi® game	1867
Lionel® train	1900
Crayola® crayons	1900
Teddy bear	1903
Rook® game	1906
Tinkertoys®	1914
Lincoln Logs®	1916
Radio Flyer® wagon	1917
LEGO® building set	1930
View-Master® 3D viewer	1938
Candy Land®	1949
Silly Putty®	1950

Toy	Year Introduced
Mr. Potato Head®	1952
Play-Doh®	1955
Barbie® doll	1959
Etch-A-Sketch®	1960
G.I. Joe®	1963
Easy Bake Oven®	1963
Twister®	1966
Spirograph®	1966
Hot Wheels® racecar set	1968
Rubik's Cube®	1979
Cabbage Patch Kids®	1983
Trivial Pursuit®	1983
Magna Doodle®	1986
Pictionary®	1987
Teenage Mutant Ninja Turtles™	1988

Yuletide Basket

WHAT YOU'LL NEED

Basket of your choice
Ribbon
Glue gun, glue sticks
Sprig of holly or poinsettia

Making a gift basket to hold your holiday goodies is easy! Make a large bow out of your favorite ribbon, wrap more ribbon around the handle, and glue ribbon around the edges of the basket. Glue a sprig of holly or poinsettia flower to the bow, and attach bow to basket. Use your imagination for additional decorating ideas!

Lemony Butter Cookies

½ cup (1 stick) butter, softened

½ cup sugar

1 egg

1½ cups all-purpose flour

2 tablespoons fresh lemon juice

1 teaspoon grated lemon peel

½ teaspoon baking powder

⅛ teaspoon salt

Additional sugar

1. Beat butter and sugar in large bowl with electric mixer at medium speed until creamy. Beat in egg until light and fluffy. Mix in flour, lemon juice, lemon peel, baking powder, and salt. Wrap in plastic wrap; refrigerate about 2 hours or until firm.

2. Preheat oven to 350°F. Roll dough, a small portion at a time, on well-floured surface to ¼-inch thickness. (Keep remaining dough in refrigerator.) Cut dough with 3-inch round or fluted cookie cutter. Transfer cutouts to ungreased cookie sheets. Sprinkle with sugar.

3. Bake 8 to 10 minutes or until edges are lightly browned. Cool 1 minute on cookie sheets. Transfer to wire racks; cool completely. Store in airtight container.

Makes about 2½ dozen cookies

Some gifts I do hope to receive,

and some to give.

Gifts immaterial, but priceless, and keyed to the tone of our times.

The gift of perspective, and a saving sense of humor.

Of capacity to appreciate the good in men without being

sentimental,

And courage to accept their faults without cynicism or despair.

The gift of understanding—not the cold kind that is brewed in

test tubes or embalmed in textbooks,

But the sympathetic understanding that springs from the heart.

—BRUCE BARTON, "THE GIFT OF UNDERSTANDING"

The best of all gifts around any Christmas tree: the presence of a happy family all wrapped up in each other.

—BURTON HILLIS

Favorite Stocking Stuffers

Candy

Nuts

Oranges

CDs and DVDs

Small stuffed animals

Playing cards

Silly Putty®

Lifesavers® Sweet Storybooks

Money

Stickers and stamps

Little dolls and toy cars

Crayons and markers

Movie tickets

Books

Lottery tickets

Lumps of coal

My first copies of *Treasure Island* and *Huckleberry Finn* still have some blue-spruce needles scattered in the pages. *They smell of Christmas still.*

—CHARLTON HESTON

Toys for Tots

In 1947 Diane Hendricks asked her husband, Bill, a major with the U.S. Marine Corps Reserves in Los Angeles, to deliver a doll she had made to an agency that gave toys to needy children at Christmastime. He soon discovered that no such agency existed, so Diane encouraged him to start one. That Christmas, Bill and a group of Marine reservists delivered 5,000 toys. The project was so successful that in 1948, the Marine Corps adopted the Toys for Tots program and extended it across the nation. And so the legendary holiday charity was born.

For the first national campaign, Walt Disney designed a poster for the program, as well as the Toys for Tots logo that is still used today. Through the years, celebrities have continued to lend their stature to the program. In 1956, Nat "King" Cole, Peggy Lee, and Vic Damone recorded a Toys for Tots theme song written by Sammy Fain and Paul Webster. Bob Hope, John Wayne, Tim Allen, and Billy Ray Cyrus are among those who have volunteered their time and talents.

Since 1947, more than 335 million toys have been delivered to nearly 160 million children in approximately 500 communities across the United States and Puerto Rico. Without a doubt, the U.S. Marines play a major role in bringing joy to America's needy children at Christmastime.

Toys for Tots continues to be a popular charity with celebrities. In 2003, the New Jersey Nets Dance Team pitched in to support the Marines in their toy drive.

In 1914, to boost sales for his new invention, Charles Pajeau hired little people, dressed them as elves, and had them play with his *Tinkertoys*® set in the display window of a Chicago department store. The merchandising ploy was overwhelmingly successful. Over the next year, more than a million sets of Tinkertoys® were sold.

Toy Trivia

- Mattel sells two Barbie® dolls per second, and 90 percent of American girls have had at least one Barbie® doll.

- The first toy advertised on television was Mr. Potato Head® in 1952. Parents had to provide children with a real potato for the body until Hasbro introduced the hard plastic body in 1964.

Game of the Century: *Monopoly®*

Toy of the Century: *LEGO®*

- In the United States, nearly 25 million hula hoops were sold in just four months during 1958 and 1959. However, the toy was banned in Japan and the USSR as a "symbol of the emptiness of American culture."

- The world's leading vehicle tire manufacturer is not Michelin or Firestone, but the LEGO Group, which produces more than 300 million tiny tires annually.

Christmas Gifts

It was Christmas Eve in the barnyard. Seven ordinary animals had just settled down for the night. It was just a typical night—or so they thought.

The hour of midnight drew near. Silent snow fell gently to the ground. And then something quite amazing happened. These seven ordinary animals, in this simple barn, became seven special animals, if only for this one night.

"What has happened?" asked the young sheep. "Baa! Baa! I can talk."

"Me, too!" said the dog. "Ruff!"

"Moo! Listen to me!" said the calf.

"What's going on?" asked the surprised donkey. "Hee-haw!"

The cow wasn't surprised. "It's midnight," she said. "And it's Christmas Eve."

"What does that mean?" asked the young sheep.

"I'll tell you a story," said the cow, "about the very first Christmas. Then you will understand."

All the animals in the barn gathered to hear the cow's story.

"Long, long ago, one special night," began the cow, "Baby Jesus was born in an ordinary stable, in an ordinary town called Bethlehem. This was the first Christmas."

"Was the stable like this barn?" the dog asked.

"Yes, almost exactly like it," said the cow.

"With animals in the stable, just like us?" asked the young calf.

"Yes," said the cow, "with animals just like us. Let me explain.

"Before Baby Jesus was born, his mother, Mary, and her husband, Joseph, had to travel through the countryside to the town of Bethle-

hem. Their trip took many days. They traveled up and down steep hills. To make things easier for Mary, an ordinary donkey carried her on his back and Joseph led the way."

"A donkey, just like me?" asked the donkey.

"Yes, a donkey just like you," said the cow.

"Finally, Mary and Joseph arrived in Bethlehem. But there was nowhere for them to sleep. They had to go to a stable and sleep with the animals. The donkey carried Mary safely to that stable.

"So it was an ordinary donkey who gave Baby Jesus a unique gift, even before he was born, by carrying Mary safely to Bethlehem.

"Later that evening, inside the simple stable, Mary gave birth to a special baby named Jesus.

"The stable was cold. Luckily, in the stable lived a handsome sheep with very soft, beautiful wool."

"A sheep, like me?" asked the young sheep.

"Yes, just like you and your mother," answered the cow. "And this sheep's soft, beautiful wool was made into a very special blanket. The sheep offered this blanket, her unique and most precious gift, to the baby. Mary wrapped Baby Jesus in this special, soft, woolly blanket. It would keep the baby snug and warm during his stay in the stable.

"After their long journey, and the birth of the baby, Mary and Joseph were too tired for lullabies. They needed something to lull the baby to sleep. But what? Mary and Joseph were lucky to find a gentle dove living high in the rafters of the stable."

"A dove, like me?" asked the dove.

"Just like you," said the cow. "And each night her soft cooing soothed the animals in the barn so they could enjoy a good night's sleep. That night was no different. The gentle dove's

lived in the stable. And though he was an ordinary dog, he was a very special watchdog."

"Just like me!" said the dog.

"Yes, just like you," said the cow. "All night, this brave dog stood watch at the door to the stable. No harm would come to Baby Jesus as long as he was around. The dog was glad to offer this precious and unique gift, and protect the baby from danger.

"All the animals in the stable gathered around Baby Jesus. Covered with a special blanket, lulled to sleep by the cooing of the dove, and protected by the dog, the baby still needed someplace special to sleep.

soft cooing quickly lulled Baby Jesus to sleep, as he lay covered with the sheep's special, soft, woolly blanket.

"But the baby still didn't have everything he needed, even with these most precious and unique gifts.

"Since Baby Jesus was so special, someone was needed to keep watch over him and his family. A brave dog

"His mother could not hold him in her arms all night. So Mary needed a comfortable bed for her child. The ordinary cow came forward and offered the manger, her most precious and unique gift, so the baby would have a safe and soft place to rest his sweet head."

"An ordinary cow, just like you and me, Mom?" asked the young calf.

"Yes, just like you and me, dear," said the cow. "Mary and Joseph lined the manger with hay and tucked the baby under the soft woolen blanket.

"That night, another special thing happened," continued the cow. "A bright star began to shine in the sky."

The animals were puzzled again.

"Where did the star come from?" asked the young calf.

"The star was a gift from God to announce to the world that a special baby had been born. It was the largest star in the sky. It shone over the earth to lead travelers from far

and near to the Baby Jesus. In fact, the star was so bright, the stable glowed as the dog stood watch, with the cow and the donkey nearby.

"So you see," said the cow, "it was on a special night, in a simple stable like this one, that ordinary animals became special animals because of the unique and most precious gifts each of them offered to Baby Jesus."

"It was a donkey, like me, who carried the baby's mother safely on his back," said the donkey.

"And a sheep, like me, gave her a special woolen blanket," said the young sheep.

"Only a dove, like me, could have lulled the baby to sleep," cooed the gentle dove.

"And it took a brave dog to keep watch over them all," said the dog, "just like me. Ruff! Ruff!"

"Yes, everyone has a unique and most special gift to give at

Christmas," said the cow. "That's why animals like us are given this special gift of speech each Christmas Eve at midnight. So we might tell our children about those very first Christmas gifts given by ordinary animals."

The animals gathered at the door to the stable. Suddenly they saw a bright star in the sky.

"Look! It's the same star!" said the young donkey.

"Yes," said the cow. "It is a special star that will always remind us of that special night when the most special baby was born."

—SUZANNE LIEURANCE

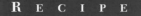
Christmas Ornament Cookies

2¼ cups all-purpose flour
¼ teaspoon salt
1 cup sugar
¾ cup (1½ sticks) butter, softened
1 egg
1 teaspoon vanilla
1 teaspoon almond extract
Icing (recipe follows)
Assorted candies and decorations

1. Place flour and salt in medium bowl; stir to blend. Beat sugar and butter in large bowl with electric mixer at medium speed until light and fluffy. Beat in egg, vanilla, and almond extract. Gradually add flour mixture. Beat at low speed until well blended. Divide dough in half; cover and refrigerate 30 minutes or until firm.

2. Preheat oven to 350°F. Working with one portion at a time, roll out dough on lightly floured surface to ¼-inch thickness. Cut dough into desired shapes with assorted floured cookie cutters. Re-roll trimmings and

cut out more cookies. Place cutouts on ungreased cookie sheets. Using drinking straw or tip of sharp knife, cut hole near top of each cookie to allow for piece of ribbon or string to be inserted for hanger. Bake 10 to 12 minutes or until edges are light brown. Let cookies stand on cookie sheets 1 minute. Remove to wire racks to cool completely.

3. Prepare icing. Spoon icing into small resealable plastic food storage bag. Cut off a very tiny corner of bag; pipe icing decoratively on cookies. Decorate with candies as desired. Let stand at room temperature 40 minutes or until set. Thread ribbon through cookie hole to hang as edible Christmas tree ornaments.

Makes about 2 dozen cookies

Icing

2 cups powdered sugar
2 tablespoons milk or lemon juice
    Food coloring (optional)

Place powdered sugar and milk or lemon juice in small bowl; stir with spoon until smooth. (Icing will be very thick. If it is too thick, stir in 1 teaspoon additional milk.) Divide into small bowls and tint with food coloring, if desired.

Abraham Lincoln's son, *Tad,* *had a warm heart.*

On Christmas Eve, 1863, he approached his father, carrying an armful of books received from his parents. The boy told his father he wanted to send them to soldiers. "Do you remember how lonesome the men looked?" Tad asked, for he had accompanied his father on camp visits. Lincoln thought for a moment before he answered proudly: "Yes, son, send a big box. Ask Mother for plenty of warm things, and tell Daniel to pack in all the good eatables he can, and let him mark the box 'From Tad Lincoln.'"

—Mrs. James S. Delano, "Recollections of the Home Life of Abraham Lincoln"

*Christmas is doing
a little something
extra for someone.*
—CHARLES SCHULZ

All Wrapped Up...

Believe it or not, Christmas gifts haven't always been presented wrapped in pretty paper. In the early days, toys and candies were dangled from the Christmas tree. In the early 1900s, presents were wrapped in white tissue paper and red satin ribbon, with a bit of holly or fresh pine tucked into the ribbon. Straight pins were used to hold the paper together until tape became the standard.

Cute Country Snow Paper

Your gift will look even better—and even more filled with love—when you make your own paper to cover it!

WHAT YOU'LL NEED

Tracing paper

Pencil

Scissors

Black marker

Sponges

Paper towels

Brown paper

Acrylic paint: white, black, brown, orange, red, green

Paper plates

Ball-head pin

Paintbrush

Kemper tool; large, stiff-bristled paintbrush; or old toothbrush

1 Photocopy or trace patterns on the following page, and cut them out. Trace patterns onto sponges with black marker, and cut out shapes. Run sponges under water, and press out excess water with paper towels.

2 Cut brown paper to desired size. Pour white paint onto a paper plate. Dip snowman sponge into paint, coating one side.

3 Sponge snowmen over the brown paper, pressing sponge onto paper. When sponge runs out of paint, reapply paint. Let snowmen dry.

4 Use black paint and hat sponge to apply hats to each snowman's head.

5 Use brown paint and twig cutout to sponge arms to sides of each snowman's body. Use orange paint and nose cutout to sponge a carrot nose onto each snowman.

6 To make facial features, dip end of ball-head pin into black paint, and dot on eyes and mouth. Use end of paintbrush to dot buttons onto each snowman. Give half the snowmen red buttons and give the other half green. Let dry completely.

7 Spatter-paint paper with white paint. To use a Kemper tool, fill bristles with white paint, hold brush over paper, and twist handle. Or, load paint-brush (or toothbrush) with white paint. Hold brush over paper, and run your finger over bristles. Let dry.

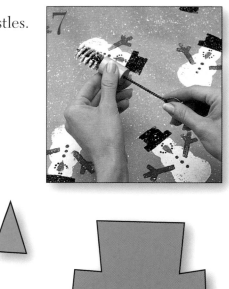

"Good King Wenceslas looked out on the Feast of Stephen, when the snow lay round about, deep and crisp and even."

King Wenceslas, about whom John Neale wrote this carol, became Duke of Bohemia in A.D. 924. He was a man of great faith who worked diligently to spread Christianity throughout Bohemia. King Wenceslas served his people very well, especially children and the poor. But his reign lasted only five years. His brother, Boleslav, invited Wenceslas to a religious festival, then attacked and murdered him on the way there.

"*The joy of brightening other lives,* bearing each others' burdens, easing others' loads and supplanting empty hearts and lives with generous gifts becomes for us the magic of Christmas."

—W. C. JONES

The History of the Christmas Card

The time-honored tradition of sending Christmas cards began more than 150 years ago in England. Sir Henry Cole, a renaissance man who wrote and published books on art and architecture, was too busy to write holiday greetings to friends and family, so he asked John Callcott Horsley, a well-known painter, to design a card with a single message that could be sent to everyone on his list.

Horsley created a lithographed, hand-colored sketch printed on cardboard. The illustration depicted a classic Victorian Christmas scene of a family merrily eating and drinking. The caption read, "A Merry Christmas and a Happy New Year to You."

The first Christmas card appeared in the United States in the mid–1800s, when New York engraver Richard Pease designed a card with a small Santa Claus, a sleigh, and reindeer. In 1875, Louis Prang, who wrote and published architectural books, printed images in color with a series of lithographic zinc plates. The finished product resembled an oil painting. These cards were so in demand that Prang couldn't fulfill all of his orders. At one point Prang was printing five million cards a year. His efforts earned him the moniker, "The Father of the American Christmas Card."

Today, everything from clever verses and holiday scenes to geometric designs and sports figures grace the fronts of cards. An average U.S. household mails out 28 Christmas cards each year and receives the same number in return. More than three billion Christmas cards are sent annually.

A MERRY CHRISTMAS
AND
A HAPPY NEW YEAR
TO YOU

Home Treasury Office
12 Old Bond Street, London.

From

Left: Richard Pease
designed the first American
Christmas card. Center:
The first known Christmas
card appeared more than
150 years ago. Right: Louis
Prang created exquisitely
detailed cards using up to
32 colors.

Toyland

Toyland! Toyland!

Little girl and boy land.

While you dwell within it—

You are ever happy then.

Childhood's joy land,

Mystic merry Toyland!

Once you pass its borders

You can never return again.

—VICTOR HERBERT,
FROM *BABES IN TOYLAND*

Christmas! The very word brings joy to our hearts. No matter how we may dread the rush, the long Christmas lists for gifts and cards to be bought and given—when Christmas Day comes there is still the same warm feeling we had as children, the same warmth that enfolds our hearts and our homes.

—JOAN WINMILL BROWN
We Wish You a Merry Christmas • 129

'Tis blessed to bestow, and yet,
Could we bestow the gifts we get,
And keep the ones we give away,
How happy were our Christmas day!

—CAROLYN WELLS

"*At this festive season of the year, Mr. Scrooge* . . .
it is more than usually
desirable that we should
make some slight provision
for the poor and destitute,
who suffer greatly at the
present time. . . . We choose
this time, because it is a
time, of all others, when
Want is keenly felt, and
Abundance rejoices."

—CHARLES DICKENS,
A CHRISTMAS CAROL

CHAPTER FOUR

Deck the Halls

Deck the halls with boughs of holly,

Fa-la-la-la-la, la-la-la-la.

'Tis the season to be jolly,

Fa-la-la-la-la, la-la-la-la.

Don we now our gay apparel,

Fa-la-la, la-la-la, la-la-la.

Troll the ancient yuletide carol,

Fa-la-la-la-la, la-la-la-la.

—Author Unknown

No one is sure exactly when or where the song *"Deck the Halls"* was written. Some scholars suggest the music originated in Wales. Others believe the lyrics are American in origin. In the Middle Ages, the *Fa-la-la-la-la* phrase was common, yet one account insists that the lyrics weren't written until after Charles Dickens's *A Christmas Carol* became popular in the 19th century. One thing is for certain: This song remains one of the best-loved carols of all time.

Holidays American Style

As in many parts of the world, Christmas is one of the most anticipated and celebrated holidays in the United States. Even before Halloween has come, many stores set out decorations and advertise holiday specials. The day after Thanksgiving, the shopping season really kicks into full gear, with stores advertising blowout sales. Families often see this as a sign to pull out decorations and begin the days-long task of decorating the house inside and out. Lights are strung around the eaves of homes. Full-size yard displays depicting Santa and his reindeer, the Nativity, and Frosty the Snowman are set up on front lawns. Inside homes, trees are wrapped with strings of lights and garland, and precious ornaments are hung from the branches. A fireplace can also be central to holiday decorating, for no home would be complete without a row of stockings waiting for Santa to stuff with tiny toys and sweet treats.

Origin of the Christmas Tree

The Christmas tree is thought to have originated in a play often performed in the Middle Ages during the Advent season. Based on the story of Adam and Eve, the play featured a Paradise Tree in the Garden of Eden that was decorated with apples to symbolize Eve's temptation. The tree used in the play was an evergreen tree, which symbolized fertility and a renewal of life. Later, in 16th century Germany, people would hang apples, gilded candies, colored paper, and roses from tree branches. Martin Luther, inspired by the beauty of stars shining through the branches of a fir tree, is credited with being the first person to add lighted candles to a tree.

Some believe that King George, a native of Germany, brought the tradition of decorating a Christmas tree to England. Others credit Queen Victoria with bringing the tradition to England from Germany where her husband, Prince Albert, was raised. An etching of the British royal family gathered around a Christmas tree in Windsor Castle in 1848 prompted the spread of this favorite decoration throughout Victorian England. The custom was brought to the United States when German immigrants in Pennsylvania continued to decorate Christmas trees just as they had done in their homeland.

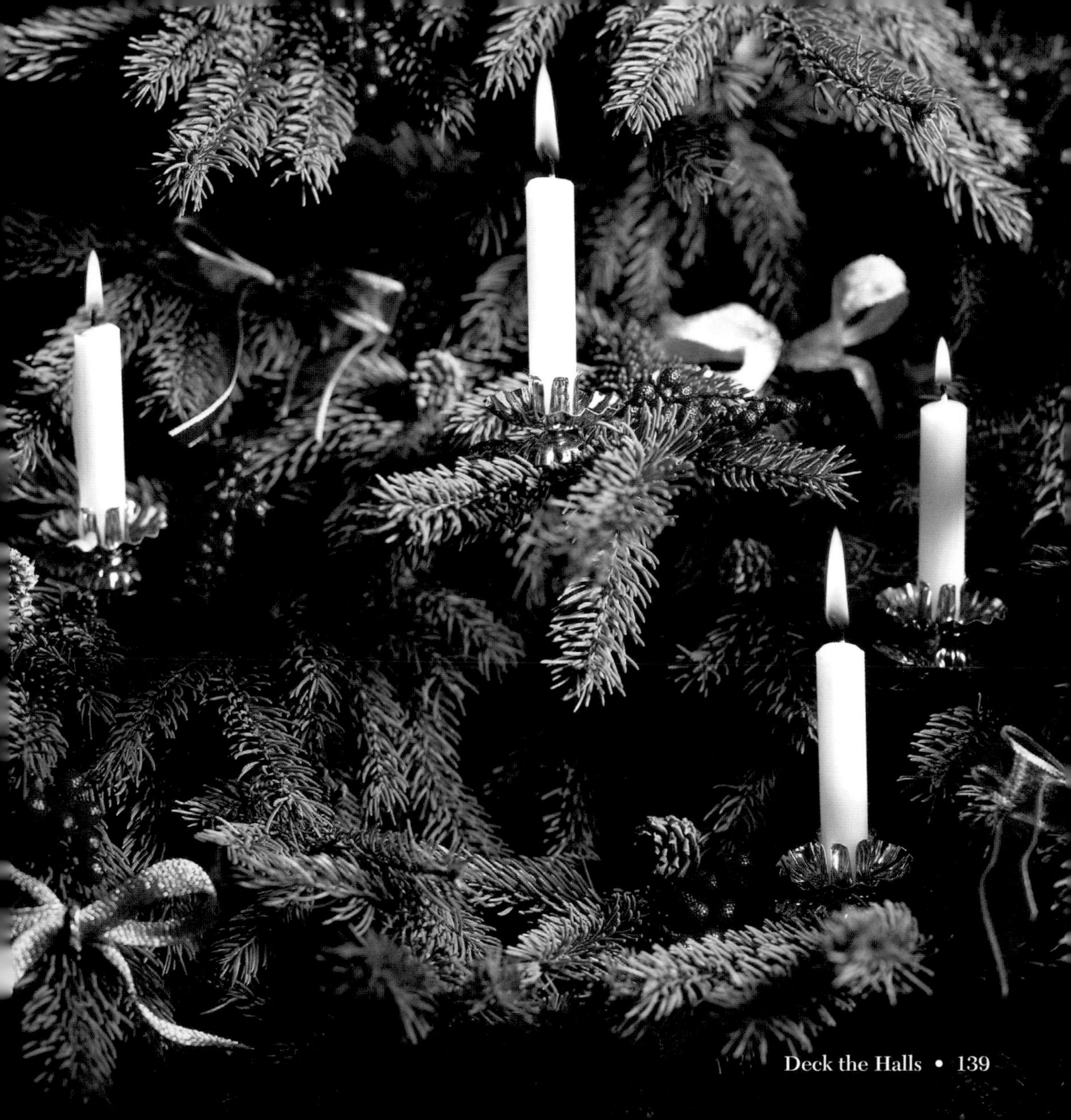

Decadent Truffle Tree

INGREDIENTS

1⅓ cups whipping cream

¼ cup packed brown sugar

¼ teaspoon salt

¼ cup light rum

2 teaspoons vanilla

16 ounces semisweet chocolate, chopped

16 ounces milk chocolate, chopped

Finely chopped nuts and assorted sprinkles

SUPPLIES

1 Foam cone (9-inch tall)

Aluminum foil

About 70 wooden toothpicks

1. Heat cream, sugar, salt, rum, and vanilla in medium saucepan over medium heat until sugar is dissolved and mixture is hot. Remove from heat; add chocolates, stirring until melted (return pan to low heat if necessary). Pour into shallow dish. Cover and refrigerate until just firm, about 1 hour.

2. Shape about half the mixture into 1¼-inch balls. Shape remaining mixture into ¾-inch balls. Roll balls in nuts and sprinkles. Refrigerate truffles until firm, about 1 hour.

3. Cover cone with foil. Starting at bottom of cone, attach larger truffles with toothpicks. Use smaller truffles toward the top of the cone. Refrigerate until serving time.

Makes 1 tree (6 dozen truffles)

NOTE: If kitchen is very warm, keep a portion of truffle mixture chilled as you shape and roll balls.

Christmas is the season for kindling the fire of hospitality in the hall, the genial flame of charity in the heart.

—Washington Irving

Holiday Botanicals

So much of Christmas decorating involves natural greenery and holiday flowers. Even if you don't have a green thumb, it is easy to incorporate these elements into your decor. All it takes to keep live and cut botanicals fresh during the holidays is tender, loving care.

It is a myth that **poinsettias** are poisonous, but they do have a bitter taste. To care for poinsettias, keep the soil moist, not wet. After the holidays, transfer the plant into a larger pot, trim the branches back once the bracts or leaves fade, and feed it every three weeks with fertilizer. As the weather warms to 60 degrees Fahrenheit, place the plant outdoors and continue trimming its branches. In October, expose the plant to 14 hours of darkness daily to force the leaves to color.

Holiday greenery such as holly, ivy, and evergreen branches will remain beautiful longer by adding a commercial floral preservative to the water. Spritz arrangements with water daily and monitor their temperature. The cooler the room, the longer the greenery stays fresh. Leaves dipped in household floor wax can last up to six weeks. This also works for decorative fruit such as grapes and pears. It gives them a shine and can keep them from spoiling for at least three weeks.

Christmas trees need water daily. Adding a commercial preservative to the water will extend the life of the tree. For a live tree, place the burlap-wrapped root-ball in a tub, and water it daily. After Christmas, dig a hole twice as large as the root-ball, carefully remove the burlap, then place the tree into the hole.

Ranging in color from red to yellow, **kalanchoes** and other succulent plants

are excellent holiday bloomers. Though the plants can withstand relatively dry conditions, keep the soil moist. After the holidays, treat kalanchoes like poinsettias, trimming the branches and feeding regularly. In the fall, allow the plant to dry out between waterings and expose it to at least 12 hours of darkness to encourage flowering.

To force **bulbs** like paperwhites, narcissus, amaryllis, and irises, plant them in October with the pointed end up in a shallow container on a layer of pebbles. Fill with sandy potting soil or with more pebbles. Water at planting time and regularly when growth begins. Place the bulbs in warm sunlight, and fertilize just before and during blooming. When flowers begin to die, reduce watering until the leaves have withered. Plant the bulbs, or place them in a cool, dark, dry place until next year.

History of the Wreath

Wreaths have a long history, dating back to ancient Druids who believed that holly, a perennial evergreen with lush, red berries, was a magical plant. Wreaths were first created when holly and other evergreens were arranged in a circular shape, a shape with no beginning or end, and therefore, synonymous with eternity. This representation took on more meaning when Jesus Christ was crowned with a wreath of thorns.

In the days of Julius Caesar, wreaths were worn by aristocrats and used by Greeks to crown victorious athletes in the original Olympic games. It is believed that hanging a wreath on a door became a custom when Olympic athletes began to hang their wreaths on their doors following a victory.

Although the word *wreath* evokes thoughts of Christmas, these lovely decorations can beautify doors and walls year-round. They can be embellished with a vast assortment of dried or artificial flowers to fit any holiday or season.

Tulip Wreath

*This beautiful wreath will carry you clear into April!
The red tulips will complement your Christmas decor
while still heralding the coming of spring
for those tired of cold days.*

WHAT YOU'LL NEED

18-inch artificial mixed evergreen wreath
3 yards sheer red ribbon, 1½ inches wide
Chenille stems
Scissors
Hot glue gun, glue sticks
8 red silk tulips with leaves
Wire cutters
3 icy branches
2 red berry sprays
Variegated ivy
Pinecones

1 Fluff wreath so it is full. Form ribbon into a multiloop bow with 5-inch loops and 18-inch streamers. Secure center of bow with chenille stem. V-cut ends of streamers.

2 Viewing wreath as a clock, glue bow to 11 o'clock position. Cut a tulip to a 10-inch stem length, and glue it to wreath so head is at 7 o'clock position.

3 Cut stems of 6 tulips to varying lengths less than 10 inches. Glue tulips above first tulip placed. Cut off stem of last tulip just below flower head, and glue it in center of bow.

4 Place icy branches among tulips. Place one berry spray among tulips and other coming out from right side of bow. Place ivy among tulips and right side of wreath. When you are pleased with the arrangement, glue everything in place.

5 Glue pinecones throughout wreath to fill in design. Make a chenille stem loop on back for hanging.

They bubble and flash, they blink and glow,

The Christmas lights we love to show,

They're blue and white and red and green,

The prettiest colors the world has seen.

We string them 'round our wreath and eaves

And light our windows, roofs, and trees,

Each bulb, so lively, bright, and gay,

The Christmas glow that lights our way.

—AUTHOR UNKNOWN

Holiday World Records

Some people love the holidays so much that they set out to break world records with their holiday cheer. For example:

- The largest Christmas stocking measures 35 feet 4½ inches long and 16 feet 5 inches wide. Created by J. Terry Osborne and friends from King William County, Virginia, it was filled with gifts to be distributed to needy children.

- Jean-Guy Laquerre of Boucherville, Quebec, Canada, is an avid Father Christmas collector, with more than 13,000 items collected since 1988. The collecting bug bit when his aunt died and left him a 12-inch-high antique papier-mâché Santa Claus from the 1920s. Since then, he has added objects such as music boxes, yo-yos, photos, candleholders, and pens.

The Perfect Tree

"The big pine trees make the prettiest trees," the little pine says to himself.

It is Christmastime in the forest, and all the trees are excited about the season. Their thick branches are covered with blankets of snow—all the branches except for the little pine's, that is.

"Who would want such a little tree with such thin branches?" he says.

"Don't worry," says the biggest spruce in the forest, "someone will think you're special."

"All trees are special," chirps a little bird, sitting on a snowy bough.

But the little pine isn't so sure. His branches droop a little.

"Hey, wait for me!" calls Sarah. "I want to pick the tree this year!"

Her brother David scoops up some soft snow and makes a snowball.

"Not if I get there first," he shouts, throwing the snowball at a lamppost.

Dad and Mom follow as the family starts out on a snowy walk to the forest.

"Remember," says Mom, "it can't be too broad, or it won't fit through the door."

"And it can't be too tall," says David, "or it will scrape the ceiling."

"We'll know the perfect tree when we see it," says Sarah.

Soon the family arrives at the forest. The trees can't wait to see which tree will be picked.

The children race right past the giant spruce trees. They stop at the little pine.

"This one!" decides Sarah.

"Yeah! It's perfect!" says David.

The children dance around the little pine.

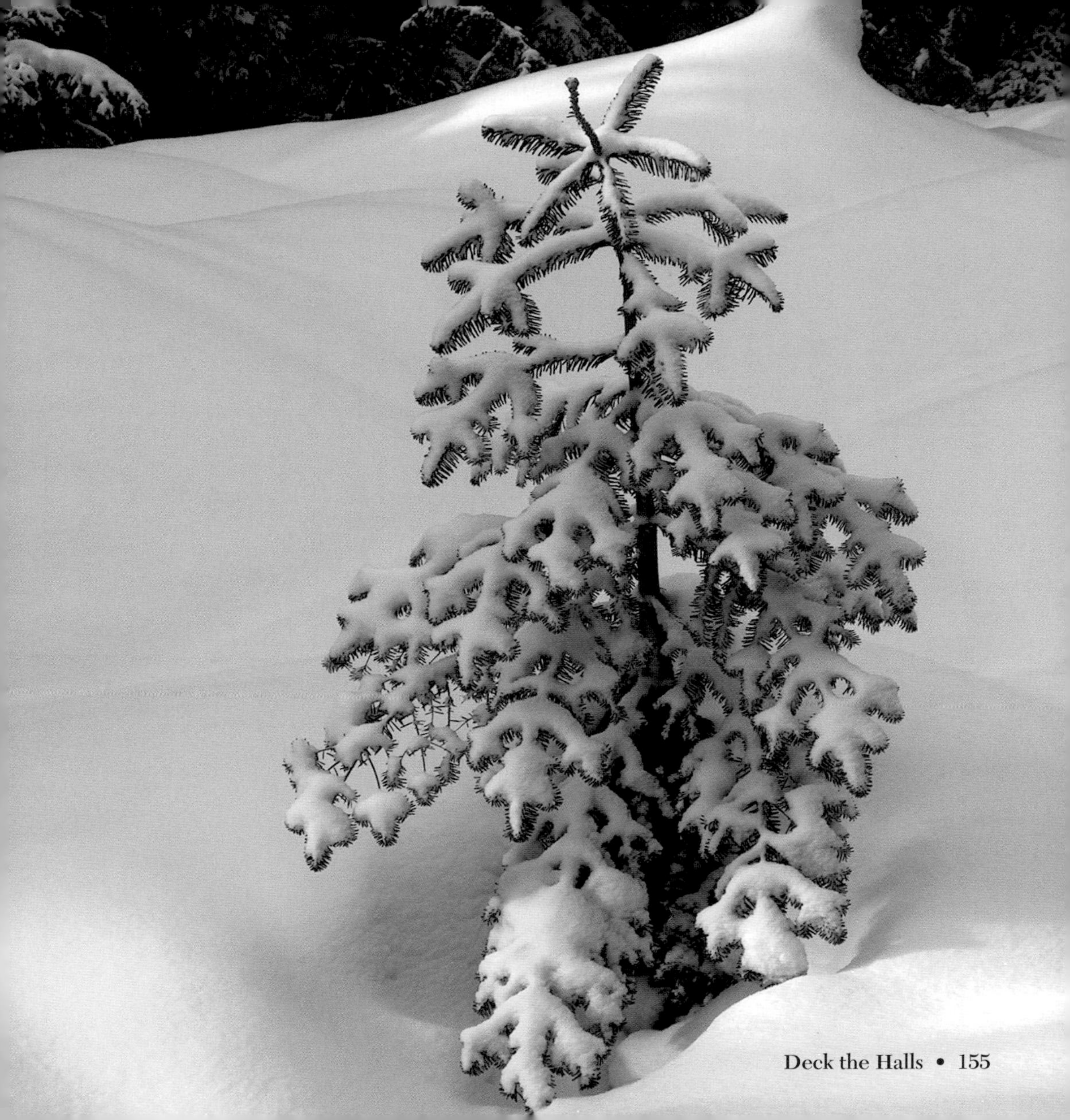

"Hmm," says Mom, "it's not too broad."

"And it won't scrape the ceiling," says Sarah.

"Looks just right to me," says Dad.

"See," says the biggest spruce, "someone thinks you're special already."

"They can't mean me," says the little pine. "Look at my thin little branches."

Dad examines the tree closely. "The trunk isn't very broad. It'll be easy to cut," he says.

"Be careful," says Mom.

"I'll be very careful," says Dad. "I won't hurt our tree a bit."

Dad begins to saw the bottom of the little pine's trunk.

"What beautiful, straight branches," says Mom. "Such a lovely little tree."

"See? They don't think your branches are skinny," says the biggest spruce. "They think you're special."

The little pine still drooped. "They think I'm special now. But wait 'til they get me home."

Once the little pine is cut, Dad carefully wraps it with twine.

"The twine makes sure the branches won't bend and break off," he tells the children.

David and Dad lead the way home with their new tree tied securely onto the sled.

"Where will we put the tree?" asks David.

"In front of the window," says Mom, "so everyone can see our perfect little tree."

"The decorations will be so beautiful!" Sarah says. "Our tree will be the best one ever!"

"I hope the decorations look right on my skinny little branches," the little pine thinks. "I don't want to disappoint my new family."

At home, Dad and David make a tree stand for the little pine. Dad puts a bowl of water at the bottom for the tree's trunk.

"What's that for?" asks David.

"To give the tree a drink," says Dad. "We need to take care of our perfect little tree."

Sarah and Mom watch as Dad and David get everything ready.

"Look," says Sarah. "People can see our tree from both front windows."

"You're right," says Mom. "Everyone will get to admire our beautiful tree."

"Oh, no," thought the little pine. "Everyone will see how silly the decorations look on me!"

Mom gets up from her chair. "Time to start decorating," she says.

"What can we do?" Sarah and David ask.

"Start with these," says Mom, scooting some boxes near the tree. Inside the box are brightly colored ornaments of all shapes and sizes.

"Ooh, they are so shiny," says Sarah.

"Some of them were Grandma's favorite ornaments," says Mom.

"What a lucky tree," says David, "to wear such special ornaments."

"I'll place the angel on the top," says Dad.

The little pine is worried the angel will not be able to balance on his thin top branches.

David and Sarah hang shiny ornaments on the little pine's branches until the boxes are empty. Mom wraps the tree with garlands of red ribbon. The angel that Dad placed atop the highest branch proudly watches over everything.

"Isn't it the most beautiful tree you have ever seen?" asks Sarah.

"It certainly is," says Dad.

"How lucky we were to find such a special tree," says David.

The little pine perks up. "The family isn't disappointed. Maybe the big spruce trees were right."

David glances out the window. "Look!" he says. "It's snowing!"

"This is the perfect Christmas," says Mom.

The little pine stands proud and straight. "The big spruce trees were right," he thinks. "Being special doesn't always mean being the biggest or the most beautiful. In the forest, I thought that I was a scrawny little pine. But now I know that I truly am special."

—SUZANNE LIEURANCE

Christmas Is in the Air

THE SIGHTS OF CHRISTMAS

Christmas trees

Snowflakes

Smiles on children's faces

Twinkling lights

THE SOUNDS OF CHRISTMAS

Crackling fire

Tearing of gift wrap

Squeals of excitement

Christmas carols

THE FEEL OF CHRISTMAS

Powdery snow

Hugs

Sting of winter chill

Warmth and softness under
Grandma's quilts

THE SMELLS OF CHRISTMAS

Gingerbread

Clean scent of a pine tree

Grandma's perfume

Aroma of cookies baking

Logs burning in the fireplace

Incense from Christmas Eve
church service

THE TASTES OF CHRISTMAS

Cool peppermint candy canes

Hot cocoa with whipped cream

Spiced eggnog

Savory turkey and stuffing

Pumpkin pie

Mulled cider

Sweet Christmas cookies

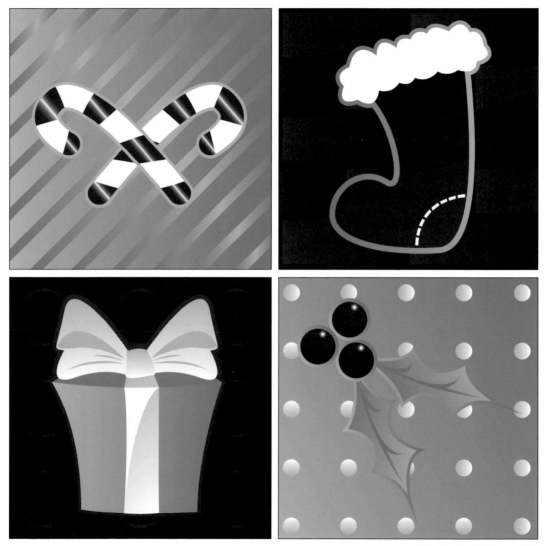

Whole Wheat Herbed Bread Wreath

4 cups all-purpose flour, divided
2 packages active dry yeast
2 tablespoons sugar
4 teaspoons dried rosemary
1 tablespoon salt
2½ cups water
2 tablespoons olive oil
3 cups whole wheat flour, divided
1 egg, beaten

1. Combine 2½ cups all-purpose flour, yeast, sugar, rosemary, and salt in large bowl. Heat water until very warm (120° to 130°F). Gradually add water and oil to flour mixture; mix until blended. Beat with electric mixer at medium speed 2 minutes. Add 1 cup whole wheat flour. Beat at high speed 2 minutes, scraping sides of bowl occasionally. By hand, stir in enough of

remaining flours to make a soft, sticky dough. Place in greased bowl; turn to grease top of dough. Cover with towel. Let rise in warm, draft-free place about 1½ hours or until doubled in size.

2. Punch down dough. Turn out onto well-floured surface. Knead about 10 minutes or until smooth and elastic. Divide into thirds. Roll each piece to form 3 24-inch ropes. Place on large greased cookie sheet. Braid ropes beginning at center and working toward ends. Seal edges. Shape into circle around greased 10-ounce, round, ovenproof bowl. Seal ends well. Cover with towel. Let rise in warm, draft-free place about 30 minutes or until doubled in size.

3. Preheat oven to 450°F. Carefully brush wreath with egg. Bake 25 to 30 minutes until wreath sounds hollow when tapped and top is golden brown. Cool on cookie sheet 10 minutes. Carefully remove from cookie sheet and bowl; cool completely on wire rack. Store tightly wrapped in plastic wrap at room temperature.

Makes one 12-inch wreath

TIP: If desired, fill center of bread with watercress, radish roses, and star-shape cutouts of flavored cheese.

One of the most glorious messes in the world is the mess created in the living room on Christmas day. *Don't clean it up too quickly.*

—ANDY ROONEY

Poinsettias

Poinsettias account for 88 percent of all plant purchases at Christmastime. The most popular color is red, but they are also available in white, cream, pink, and yellow, and they can be striped, spotted, or marbled. Originating in Mexico, where they are known as the "Flower of the Holy Night," the flowers were brought to the United States by Joel Poinsett in 1829. In their native country, they grow as shrubs and can reach heights up to ten feet tall. In Mexico, a heart-warming story explains the origin of the poinsettia:

> On a Christmas Eve, long ago, a poor little boy went to church in great sadness because he had no gift to bring the Holy Child. He dared not enter the church, and, kneeling humbly on the ground outside the house of God, he prayed fervently and assured our Lord, with tears, how much he desired to offer him some lovely present—"But I am very poor and dread to approach you with empty hands." When he finally rose from his knees, he saw springing up at his feet a green plant with gorgeous blooms of dazzling red.

—Francis X. Weiser

Cross-Stitch Bread Cloth

This lovely handmade bread cloth will not only dress up your homemade bread, it will keep it warm for everyone to enjoy!

WHAT YOU'LL NEED

White 14-count bread cover
6-strand embroidery floss (see color key)
#8 gold fine braid
#24 tapestry needle
Scissors

Stitch Count: 50h×50w
Size: 3⅝×3⅝ inches

COLOR KEY:

Ultra very dark emerald ■
Emerald green dark ■
Christmas red ■
Light Christmas red ■
Gold ■

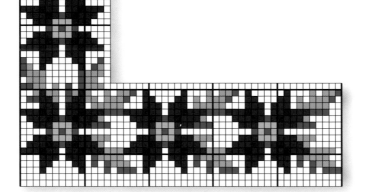

Cross-stitch design in a corner of bread cover, ½ inch from fringed edge. Use 2 strands floss and 1 strand fine braid.

Until one feels the spirit of Christmas,
there is no Christmas.

All else is outward display—so much tinsel and decorations.

For it isn't the holly, it isn't the snow.

It isn't the tree, not the firelight's glow.

It's the warmth that comes to the hearts of men

When the Christmas spirit returns again.

—ANONYMOUS (PIPEFULS)

Holly

For centuries, holly has been synonymous with the holiday season. In ancient Rome, holly branches were given as a gesture of friendship during Saturnalia, the winter solstice festival. Druids would decorate their homes with holly during Britain's gloomy winters, believing that the sun always shone on this sacred tree. Likewise, pagans would bring holly and other evergreens inside to ensure that Nature would return in the spring.

There are hundreds of species of holly that can be clipped and used in seasonal decorations. Perhaps the most well known is American holly, which features spiny, glossy leaves and bright red berries. Inkberry holly, named for its deep purple-black berries, and variegated holly, with striped leaves, are striking alternatives to the standard holiday holly.

May the fire of this log

warm the cold;

May the hungry be fed;

May the weary find rest,

And may all enjoy

Heaven's peace.

—TRADITIONAL PRAYER SAID
WHEN YULE LOG IS LIT

Pucker Up!

Who doesn't love hanging mistletoe? Although most mistletoe is parasitic, and, therefore, harmful to the trees on which it grows, the Celts thought it had magical powers for healing wounds and increasing fertility, so they placed it throughout their homes for good luck and to ward off evil spirits. In ancient Britain, mistletoe was considered so sacred that it could only be cut with a golden sickle. Today, Americans decorate door frames with this plant in hopes of catching a smooch from a sweetheart while standing under its leaves. This tradition is credited to Frigga, the Scandinavian goddess of love and beauty, and is said to date back to the eighth century.

The National Christmas Tree

America's official national Christmas tree is not located at the White House, but rather in King's Canyon National Park near Sanger, California. The tree, a giant sequoia known as the General Grant Tree, was designated the "Nation's Christmas Tree" in 1925. It is 267 feet high, 40 feet across its base, and is estimated to be between 1,500 and 2,000 years old. In 1956, the tree was declared a national shrine to honor the men and women of the U.S. military. As a memorial, park

rangers place a wreath at the base of the tree during the Christmas ceremony, which has been held every year since 1925.

Get Your Message Across

This simple Scandinavian-style garland is sure to dress any bare window with holiday cheer. To make your own, you'll need manila office tags with reinforced holes, alphabet stamps, a stamp pad, and jute. Lay the office tags on a flat surface, one for each letter of your message. Press a letter into the stamp pad then onto the center of a tag and let dry. Cut a piece of jute twice the length desired. Working from the middle of the jute, string each tag onto the jute individually, and tie into place with a small piece of jute. When all tags are secured, stretch the jute garland across a window or mantel, and fasten in place with thumbtacks or tape.

A Christmas candle is a lovely thing;
It makes no noise at all,
But softly gives itself away;
While quite unselfish, it grows small.

—Eva K. Logue

The holly and the ivy

When they are both full grown,

Of all the trees that are in the wood

The holly bears the crown.

—AUTHOR UNKNOWN,
FROM "THE HOLLY AND THE IVY"

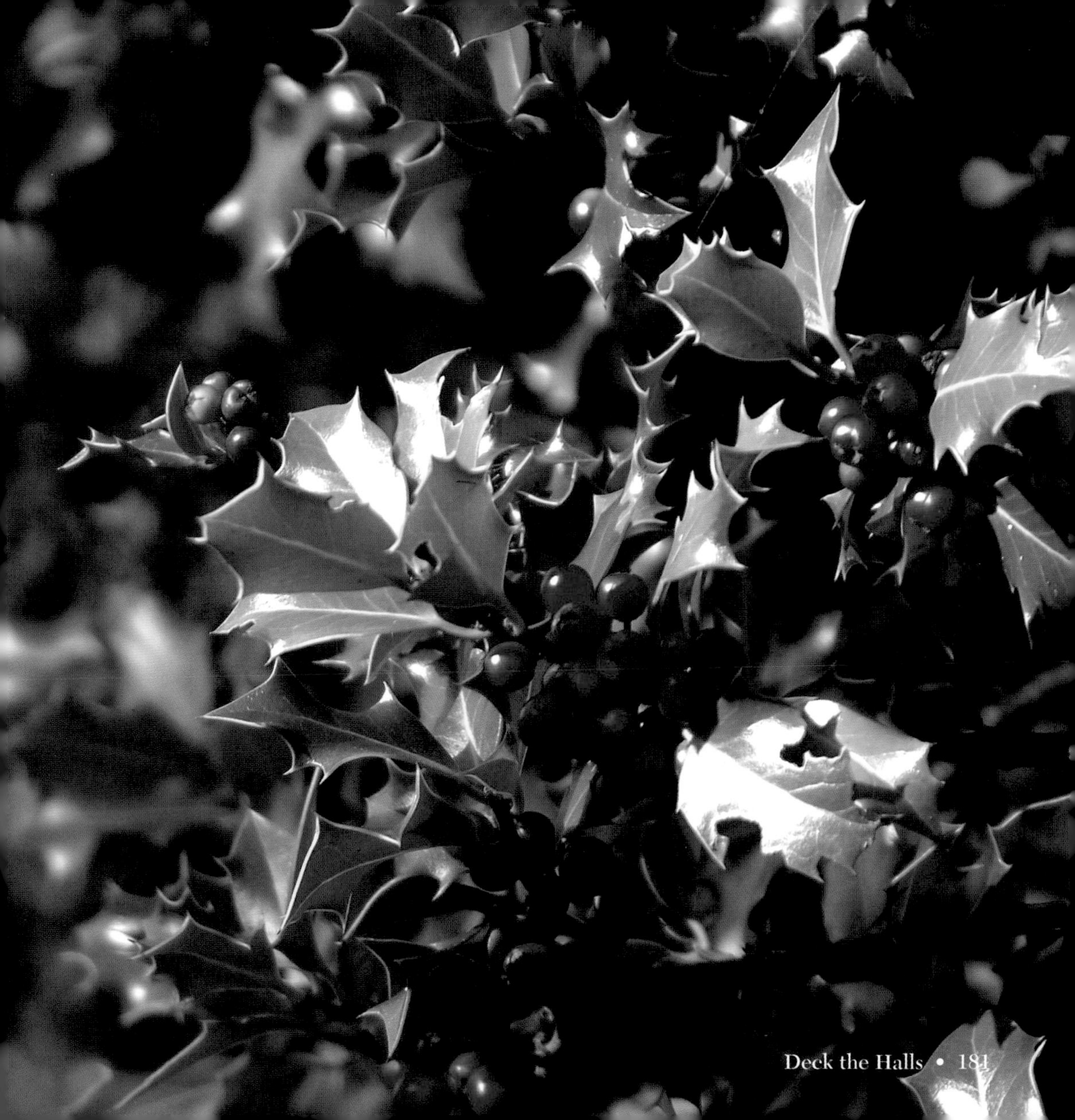

CHAPTER FIVE

Joy to the World

Joy to the world!

The Lord is come;

Let earth receive her King.

Let ev'ry heart prepare Him room,

And heav'n and nature sing,

And heav'n and nature sing,

And heav'n and heav'n and nature sing.

—ISAAC WATTS

In 1719, when Isaac Watts wrote the words to *"Joy to the World,"* his inspiration was Psalm 98: "Make a joyful noise unto the Lord, all the earth . . . " Surprisingly, the song was not immediately accepted, as many felt Watts was trying to improve upon the Scriptures.

It is believed that after Watts's death, Lowell Mason set the lyrics to the music we know today, which was taken from several sources, including Handel's *Messiah.* In the 19th century, Mason published "Joy to the World," which he renamed "Antioch," for the city in Syria where followers of Jesus were first called Christians.

What's for Christmas Dinner in America?

Baked ham

Turkey and stuffing

Mashed potatoes and gravy

Sweet potatoes

Green bean casserole

Winter squash soup

Waldorf salad

Cranberry salad

Parker house rolls

Divinity

Red velvet cake

Pumpkin pie

Talking Turkey

- The largest turkey on record weighed 86 pounds, about the size of a large dog.
- Native Americans used turkey feathers to stabilize arrows.
- Twenty-two million turkeys are consumed each year at Christmas, compared to 45 million at Thanksgiving.
- On average, each American eats more than 17 pounds of turkey annually.

The Cratchits' Christmas Dinner

Bob said he didn't believe there ever was such a goose cooked. Its tenderness and flavour, size and cheapness, were the themes of universal admiration. Eked out by applesauce and mashed potatoes, it was a sufficient dinner for the whole family; indeed, as Mrs. Cratchit said with great delight (surveying one small atom of a bone upon the dish), they hadn't ate it all at last! Yet everyone had had enough, and the youngest Cratchits in particular, were steeped in sage and onion to the eyebrows! But now, the plates being changed by Miss Belinda, Mrs. Cratchit left the room alone—too nervous to bear witnesses—to take the pudding up and bring it in.

Suppose it should not be done enough? Suppose it should break in turning out? Suppose somebody should have got over the wall of the backyard, and stolen it, while they were merry with the goose—a supposition at which the two young Cratchits became livid! All sorts of horrors were supposed.

A great deal of steam. The pudding was out of the copper. A smell like a washing-day. That was the cloth. A smell like an eating-house and a pastry-cook's next door to each other, with a laundress's next door to that. That was the pudding. In half a minute Mrs. Cratchit entered—flushed, but smiling proudly—with the pudding, like a speckled cannon-ball, so hard and firm, blazing in half of half-a-quartern of ignited brandy, and bedight with Christmas holly stuck into the top.

Oh, a wonderful pudding. Bob Cratchit said, and calmly too, that he

Mrs. Cratchit serves her family Christmas dinner in the Muppets' adaptation of A Christmas Carol.

regarded it as the greatest success achieved by Mrs. Cratchit since their marriage. Mrs. Cratchit said that now the weight was off her mind, she would confess she had had her doubts about the quantity of flour. Everybody had something to say about it, but nobody thought or said it was at all a small pudding for a large family. It would have been flat heresy to do so. Any Cratchit would have blushed to hint at such a thing.

—CHARLES DICKENS
FROM *A CHRISTMAS CAROL*

What Is Figgy Pudding Anyway?

Before you sing, "Now bring us some figgy pudding," it might be helpful to know exactly what you are requesting. Figgy pudding is an English dish similar to bread pudding. Made from figs, bread crumbs, cinnamon, nutmeg, and milk, the pudding is baked, then topped with a scrumptious brandied hard sauce, custard icing, powdered sugar, or whipped cream. The dish was immortalized in the song "We Wish You a Merry Christmas" and was served by Mrs. Cratchit in the Charles Dickens classic *A Christmas Carol.*

*How bless'd,
how envied,
were our life,*

Could we but 'scape the
poulterer's knife!

But man, curs'd man,
on Turkeys preys,

And Christmas shortens
all our days:

Sometimes with oysters
we combine,

Sometimes assist the
savory chine;

From the low peasant
to the lord,

The Turkey smokes on
every board.

—JOHN GAY

Boxing Day:

A FESTIVE FEAST IN ENGLAND

Although the exact origin of Boxing Day is unknown, it is believed to date back to England during the Middle Ages. The most widely accepted theory is that even though servants were required to work on Christmas Day, they were given a reprieve the day after to visit family, with their employers sending them off with a box containing gifts and food, hence the term "Boxing Day." Today, people continue to celebrate by taking the day off to visit family and friends and to give presents to those who have helped them throughout the year.

Traditional Christmas festivities in England include tables laden with pine boughs, holly, mistletoe, juniper berries, cinnamon sticks, oranges with fragrant cloves, bowls of fruit, and tiny Christmas trees scattered throughout. Party favors are placed on plates. These include English "crackers," which are colored paper tubes filled with candy and small gifts. The typical English Christmas feast consists of:

- Pheasant or chicken
- Turkey
- Assorted sausages
- Stuffing
- Roasted potatoes
- Yams
- Filo crackers
- Mince pies
- Poached pears
- Scones and muffins with berry butter
- Christmas (plum) pudding
- Fruitcake

Fruity Over Fruitcake—Or Not!

Fruitcake \früt-kāk\ *n* (1848) 1: a rich cake containing nuts, dried or candied fruits, and spices; 2: a foolish, eccentric, or crazy person.

What is Christmas without fruitcake? Indeed, this chewy, rich confection is a staple of the holidays, but what, *exactly,* is it? It is called a cake, but because it is chock-full of nuts and candied fruits, it resembles a candy bar. When sliced, pieces can be passed off as cookies.

In ancient times, fruitcake was made with raisins, pomegranate seeds, and pine nuts mixed together with barley mash. Later, honey, spices, and candied fruits were added. Because of fruitcake's consistency and longevity, early warriors and hunters carried it with them on long journeys.

In the 1700s, Europeans baked ceremonial fruitcakes at the end of the nut harvest, saved them, and then ate them at the beginning of the *next* year's harvest. This was done with the hope that it would bring another successful harvest. Also, throughout Europe during this time, the consumption of fruitcake (also called plum cake) was restricted to special occasions because of its "sinfully rich" taste. Those laws were later rescinded, and fruitcake became an essential of the Victorian tea era.

In 18th-century England, it was believed that unmarried wedding guests who put a slice of fruitcake under their pillow at night would dream of the person they were destined to marry.

Feliz Navidad

Mexicans celebrate the birth of Jesus with *las Posadas*, nine days of preparation during which the story of the Nativity is reenacted each day. These days lead up to *Noche Buena* (Holy Night) or Christmas Eve. Most families go to mass, then head home for dinner with family and friends. The highlight of the evening is placing Baby Jesus in the manger in the Nativity scene.

To prepare for the celebration, the house is decorated with pottery; bowls of fruit; brightly colored paper ornaments; colorful confetti; tinsel-trimmed maracas; star-shaped piñatas filled with oranges, tangerines, peanuts, and candy canes; red, green, and silver tablecloths; small lanterns and candles; and, of course, a Nativity scene.

The spread for Feliz Navidad includes:

- Roast turkey, ham, or suckling pig
- Biscayan cod
- Tamales
- Stuffed chili peppers
- Wild greens in mole sauce
- Atole (beverage made from corn)
- Chili con queso with chips
- Guacamole with flakes of red bell pepper "confetti"
- Ensalada de Navidad (Christmas fruit salad)
- Sidra (sparkling cider)
- Chocolate atole (cinnamon hot chocolate)
- Ponche con piquete (hot punch of fruits and cinnamon sticks)
- Bizcochos (holiday cookies)
- Sweet Christmas fritters
- Flan

Holiday Star

TOPPING

¾ cup sour cream

½ cup mayonnaise

2 tablespoons heavy cream

1 teaspoon balsamic vinegar

¼ cup chopped fresh cilantro

¼ cup chopped fresh basil

¼ cup chopped roasted red pepper,
drained and patted dry

½ teaspoon garlic powder

¼ teaspoon salt

Black pepper to taste

STAR

2 cans (8 ounces each) refrigerated crescent
roll dough

GARNISHES

Chopped red bell pepper, chopped green
onion, and sliced black olives

1. Preheat oven to 375°F.

2. For topping, combine sour cream, mayonnaise, cream, and vinegar in medium bowl. Stir in cilantro, basil, and roasted red pepper. Add garlic powder, salt, and black pepper; mix well. Cover and refrigerate at least 1 hour or until ready to use to let flavors blend.

3. For star, place 2-inch round cookie cutter or custard cup in center of ungreased 14-inch pizza pan; set aside. Remove dough from one can; unroll onto waxed paper. Seal perforations by pressing down lightly with fingers. Cut out 24 circles with 1½-inch round cookie cutter. Remove excess dough from cut circles; set aside. Repeat with second can.

4. Evenly space five dough circles around outside edge of pizza pan. (These will be the star points.) From each star point, make triangular pattern with rows of slightly over-lapping dough circles, working toward cookie cutter in center of pan. Roll excess dough into ball; flatten with hands. Cut more circles as needed to completely fill star.

5. Remove cookie cutter from center of star. Bake 12 to 16 minutes or until star is light golden brown. Cool completely in pan on wire rack, about 30 minutes.

6. Spread topping over star. Garnish with red bell pepper, green onion and black olive slices. Place decorative candle in center of star, if desired. Serve immediately.

Makes about 16 servings

TIP: For a festive garnish, hollow out a red or green bell pepper and fill it with any remaining dip. Place fresh vegetables, such as broccoli florets or bell pepper strips, around the star.

The Legend of Bûche de Noël

A classic French dessert, *Bûche de Noël* is a delicious confection of chocolate cake and rich pastry cream rolled into the shape of a log. The cake symbolizes the belief that a large log should burn continuously on Christmas night. If it goes out, it means bad luck in the coming year. The next morning, the ashes from the log are scooped up and kept as a good luck charm to heal sickness, bring on needed rain, and guarantee success in business.

Will Santa Come for Christmas Dinner?

I first saw him at our friends' wedding rehearsal. The resemblance was uncanny. There was no red suit with white fur trim, no fat belly, and no sleigh and reindeer. But the beard was the purest white I had ever seen. It was the most authentic Santa beard anyone could conceive. My adult mind kept playing a childish refrain. "It's Santa! It's really Santa!"

How appropriate that the wedding would be on December 23. Santa was to provide the music. He was rather solemn as the others celebrated in a festive mood. The minister showed him where to stand during the ceremony. I assumed he would sing. But the thin, bearded Santa in blue jeans reached down, opened a violin case, and lovingly took out his instrument.

Santa was not just a man playing a violin. It was obvious even to the untrained ear that the strings were in the hands of a master. People who had been chatting in various parts of the church slipped into the pews one by one, moved by the talent of this quiet gentleman.

He sat across the table from me at the rehearsal dinner. He did look like Santa, but carrying on a conversation with him was quite difficult. I learned that he was a plumber, not a professional musician, and that there was no "Mrs. Claus." He would be spending Christmas alone.

The idea preyed on my mind all night. Santa spending Christmas alone? The next day I asked the bride-to-be, "What's with Santa? No

twinkle in his eye, no family, and no one to spend Christmas with?" She looked at me. "You don't know, do you?"

I instantly knew that I was not prepared for her answer. She said that Santa had loved his wife and son very much—he was a devoted husband and father. Several years ago, he came home from work in early December to find them both gone—their lives snuffed out by an intruder. He hasn't been the same since. There is no twinkle in his eyes. And he can't bear to hold little children and listen to their precious requests as he had done for so many years. No more Santa in the red suit—just the plumber in blue jeans.

At the reception, he stood all alone. I did manage to engage him in some small talk. "Yes, it was a beautiful wedding." I looked him in the eye. "Will you come to our house for Christmas dinner?" His face flushed. I could see his hands shaking. "We have five sons. May I tell them Santa is coming for Christmas dinner?" I slipped him a note with our address. He stared into space. I turned away unacknowledged.

As I tucked the younger boys in bed on Christmas Eve, I spoke softly. "Maybe we will have a special guest for dinner tomorrow. Who knows? Maybe Santa himself will be here!"

I prayed as I laid my head on the pillow. "Please don't let Santa be alone on Christmas."

The turkey was browned perfectly. The desserts were arranged on a special table, and everyone was starving. One o'clock and time for dinner. That morning, each of the boys, one by one, had come to ask me. "Mom, did you really invite him?" "Do you think he's going to come?"

My answer: "I hope so, Son."

We couldn't wait any longer. "Time for Christmas dinner!" Everyone gathered around the table. I saw the disappointment in the boys' faces. But just as the "amen" at the end of the blessing was pronounced, we all heard a car door slam. The boys raced to the back door. I could tell by the amazement on their faces who was coming up the back steps. "Mom, it's him! It's him! It's really Santa Claus—in his everyday clothes, the ones he must wear all year in his workshop!"

The boys never saw the tears I brushed away as they rushed to welcome Santa into our home. After we opened our presents (there were even two for Santa), Santa spoke. "May I give your family a gift now?"

He went outside and came back with his old black violin case. As he played, I was sure I could hear angels joining in as we sang "Silent Night."

After he put the instrument away, our two-year-old toddled over to Santa and gently stroked his beard. "Santa, tan I sits on ur lap?" I saw all the color drain from Santa's cheeks. For a moment, he was as white as his beard. Then slowly, slowly, Santa eased back into his big chair, and finally he stretched out his arms.

—Elaine Slater Reese

Swedish Holiday Traditions

On December 13, one of the darkest days of the year, St. Lucia Day, or the Festival of Lights, is celebrated throughout Sweden to symbolize the promise of the sun's return. In the past, a young girl would dress in a white gown with a red sash and a wreath of lit candles on her head. She would go from house to house offering baked goods. Today, the tradition continues with the oldest girl in a family wearing the traditional dress with a wreath of (battery-powered) candles on her head, awakening everyone with a song and saffron buns and coffee.

According to legend, Lucia was a young girl that lived during the fourth century. She was blinded for her Christian beliefs. St. Lucia is the patron saint of the blind.

For a Swedish Christmas dinner, sit down to a table of:

- Ham
- Lutefisk (fish soaked in lye)
- Boiled wheat (*cuccidata*)
- Cabbage pudding
- Baby potatoes
- Sweet carrots
- Medley of vegetables
- Deviled eggs
- Julglögg (a hot, mulled wine)
- Fruit salad
- Saffron buns with raisins
- Rice pudding
- Lingonberry pie
- Broomstick cookies (a lacy cookie with almonds and butter)
- Pepparkakor (sweet ginger cookies)

St. Lucia Bread Wreath

INGREDIENTS

1 to 1½ teaspoons ground cardamom

1 package (16 ounces) hot roll mix, plus
  ingredients to prepare mix

½ recipe Cookie Glaze (page 210)

Red and green candied cherries

SUPPLIES

Small custard cup

Artificial holly leaves* (optional)

5 candles, 7 or 8 inches each

Real holly leaves are toxic; do not use on food.

1. Stir cardamom into hot roll mix. Prepare mix according to package directions. Knead dough on lightly floured surface until smooth, about 5 minutes. Cover loosely; let stand in bowl about 15 minutes.

2. Grease large baking sheet and outside of custard cup. Place inverted custard cup in center of prepared baking sheet; set aside.

3. Punch down dough; divide into 3 equal pieces. On floured surface, roll and stretch 2 pieces of dough into 20-inch ropes. Twist ropes together; shape into 7-inch circle around custard cup.

4. Divide remaining dough piece in half. Place dough on floured surface; roll and stretch each piece into 12-inch rope. Twist 2 ropes together; shape into 5-inch circle. Place around custard cup, overlapping top of larger braid already on baking sheet.

5. To make holes for candles, shape small sheets of foil into 5 balls, each 1 inch in diameter. Insert balls between 2 braids, evenly spacing them around wreath. Cover dough loosely; let rise in warm place until doubled in bulk, 20 to 30 minutes.

6. Preheat oven to 375°F. Prepare Cookie Glaze.

7. Uncover dough. Bake 25 to 30 minutes or until golden brown. Remove custard cup. Cool wreath on wire rack. Drizzle Cookie Glaze over wreath; decorate with cherries and artificial holly leaves, if desired. Before serving, remove balls of foil. Wrap bottoms of candles with small pieces of additional foil; insert candles into holes. *Makes 8 to 10 servings*

COOKIE GLAZE: Combine 4 cups powdered sugar and 4 tablespoons milk in small bowl. Stir; add 1 to 2 tablespoons more milk as needed to make pourable glaze.

The darkness shall
  soon depart
from the earth's valleys
thus she speaks
a wonderful word to us.
The day shall rise anew
from the rosy sky.
Saint Lucia,
Saint Lucia.

—AUTHOR UNKNOWN

Christmas Trivia

- Barnum's animal crackers in the circus-themed box were designed with a string handle so they could hang on a Christmas tree.
- Sugarplums are actually chocolate candies with cream, fruit preserves, or other sweet fillings inside.
- Wassail is a beverage dating back to the Middle Ages. The word is derived from the Old Norse *ves heill*, meaning "in good health." This evolved into visiting neighbors on Christmas Eve and drinking to their health. Traditional wassail contained ale, wine, or hard cider topped with beaten eggs or stale bread. Modern recipes for wassail use hot apple cider simmered with spices and sweetened with honey.
- The first candy canes were straight, white sticks of sugar candy used as Christmas tree decorations. In 1670, a choirmaster in Cologne, Germany, bent the ends to resemble a shepherd's staff and handed them out to children during church services to keep them quiet. In the early 1900s, candy canes acquired their famous stripes.
- Eating mincemeat pie on Christmas dates back to the 16th century. Traditionally, it was thought that eating a small pie on each of the 12 days of Christmas would bring good luck in the new year.

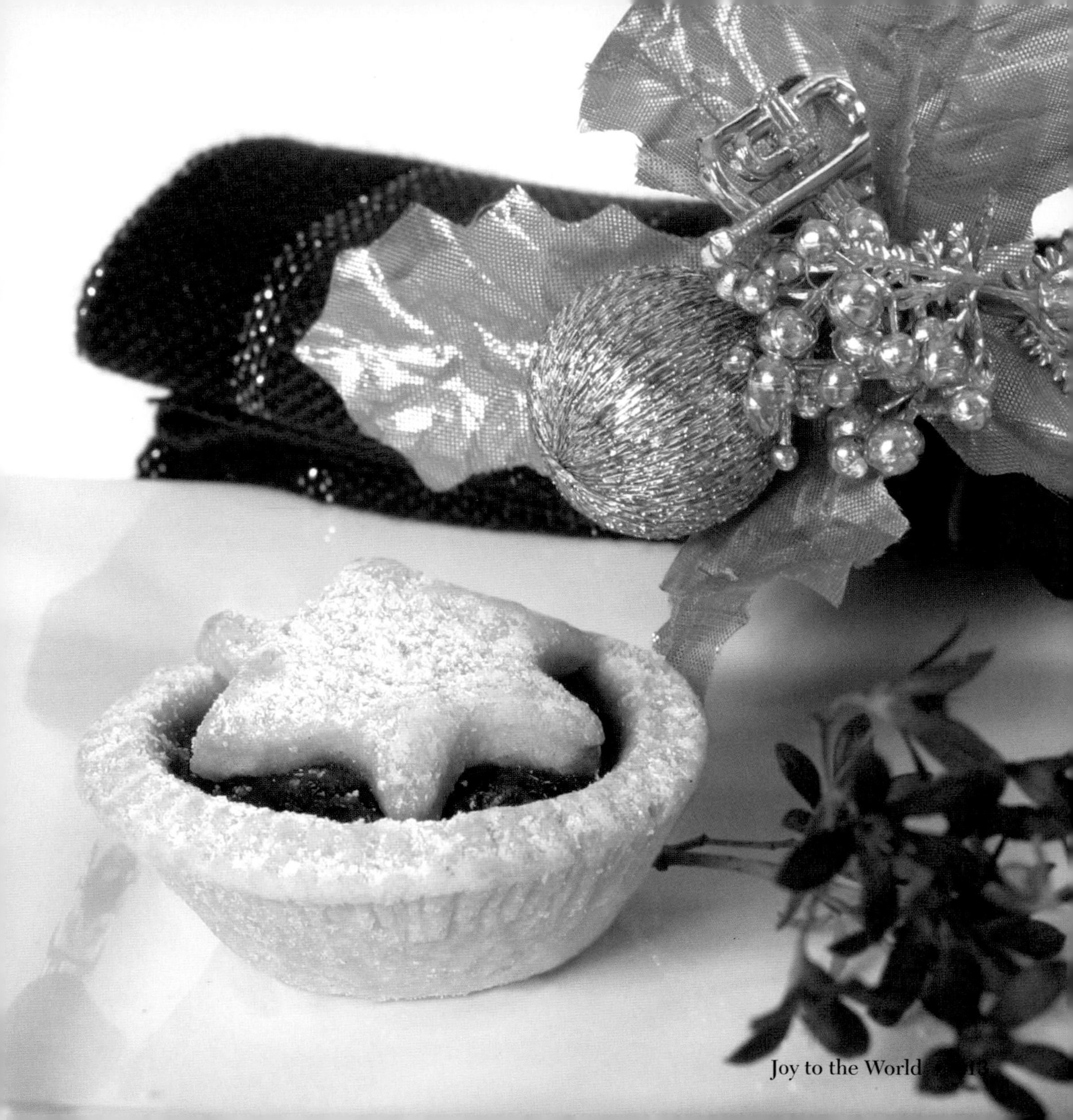

An Old-World Christmas in Germany

Celebrating the season is a month-long event in Germany, with festivities culminating on Christmas Eve, when the Christmas tree is unveiled. Children are not allowed to see the tree until a bell rings to signify that the Christ Child has been there. Once the tree is revealed, fully decorated with tinsel, lights, and ornaments, families place presents underneath and sing Christmas carols. The night later gives way to a feast so lavish that the evening is often called *dickbauch,* or "fat stomach." It is believed that those who do not eat well will be haunted by demons during the night. Nuts, fruits, marzipan, greenery, candles, and adorable carved, wooden figurines of angels, trees, and Santa are placed around the table. The night's delights include:

- Roasted goose
- Ham or suckling pig
- White sausage
- Sausage and cheese bread
- Roasted potatoes
- Green beans
- Yams
- Macaroni salad
- Rice porridge
- Biscuits and marmalade
- Fruit salad
- Apple cider
- Christstollen (bread with nuts, raisins, and dried fruit)
- Lebkuchen (gingerbread)
- Marzipan

Gingerbread

Whether baked into delicious spiced cakes or crunchy, flat cookies, or used to build a "house," gingerbread has been a European delicacy for centuries. As the dessert spread throughout Western Europe, gingerbread became a part of local traditions. In England, unmarried women would eat gingerbread "husbands" for luck in meeting the real thing. On festival days, images of saints would be stamped in gingerbread and sometimes iced.

Today, gingerbread is often associated with Germany and its holiday traditions. Gingerbread hearts are commonly found at fall fairs, decorated with colored icing and tied with ribbons. In December in Nuremburg, the "gingerbread capital of the world," the *Christkindlmarkt* features the famous *lebkuchen,* which is considered to be the best gingerbread in the world.

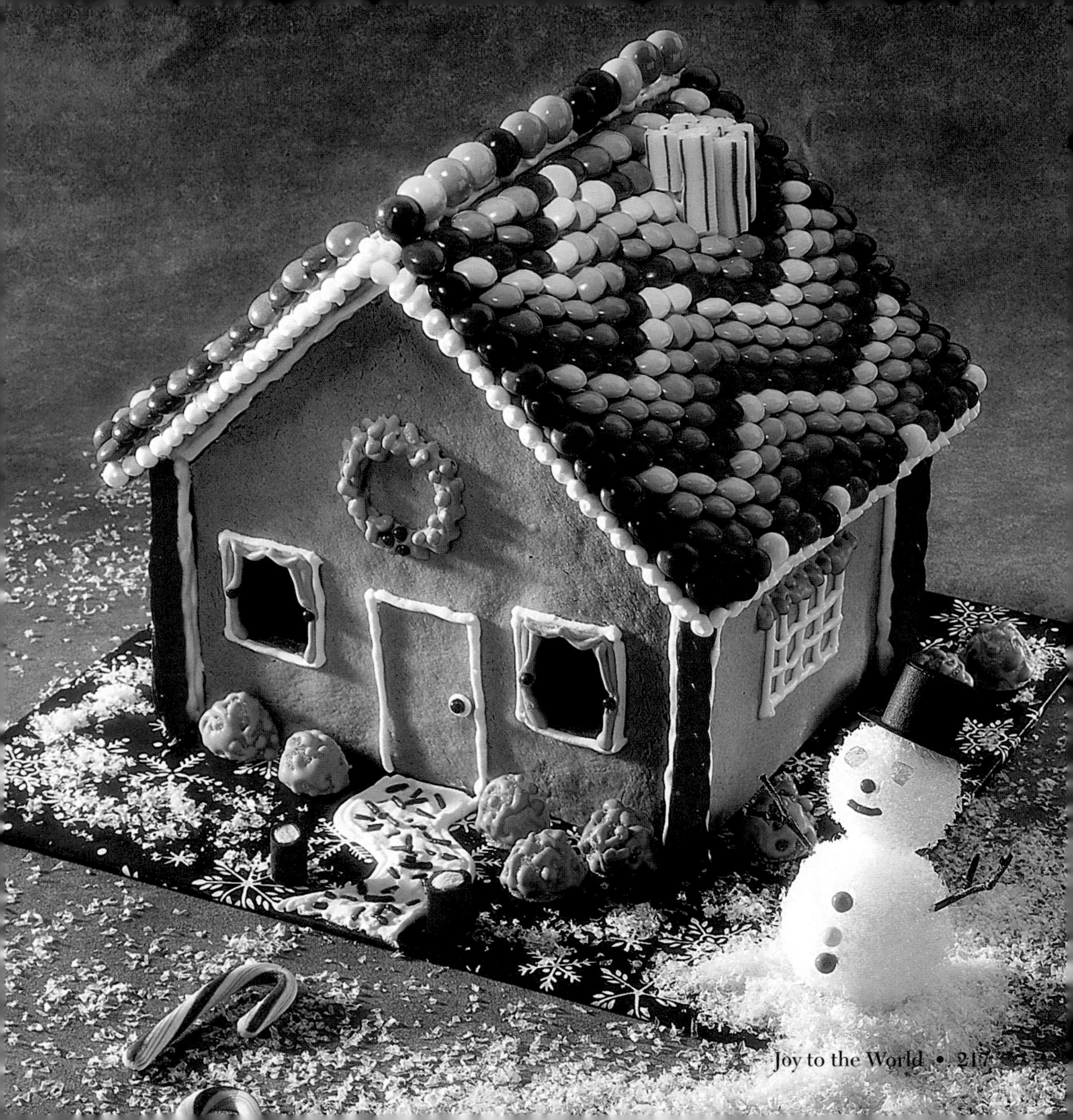

Chocolate Gingerbread Cookies

½ cup (1 stick) butter, softened

½ cup packed light brown sugar

¼ cup granulated sugar

1 tablespoon shortening

4 squares (1 ounce each) semisweet chocolate, melted and cooled

2 tablespoons molasses

1 egg

2¼ cups all-purpose flour

3 tablespoons unsweetened cocoa powder

2½ teaspoons ground ginger

½ teaspoon baking soda

½ teaspoon ground cinnamon

⅛ teaspoon salt

⅛ teaspoon finely ground black pepper

Prepared icing (optional)

1. Beat butter, sugars, and shortening in large bowl with electric mixer at medium speed until creamy. Add chocolate; beat until blended. Add molasses and egg; beat until well blended. Combine flour, cocoa, ginger, baking soda, cinnamon, salt, and pepper in medium bowl. Gradually add flour mixture to butter mixture, beating until well blended. Divide dough in half. Wrap each half in plastic wrap; refrigerate at least 1 hour.

2. Preheat oven to 350°F. Roll out half of dough between sheets of plastic wrap to about ¼-inch thickness. Cut out shapes with 5-inch cookie cutters; place cutouts on ungreased cookie sheets. Refrigerate at least 15 minutes. Repeat with remaining dough.

3. Bake 8 to 10 minutes or until cookies have puffed slightly and have small crackles on surfaces. Cool 5 minutes on cookie sheets; remove to wire racks to cool completely. Decorate cooled cookies with icing, if desired. *Makes about 2 dozen 5-inch cookies*

CHEWY CHOCOLATE GINGERBREAD DROPS: Decrease flour to 1¾ cups. Shape 1½ teaspoonfuls of dough into balls. Place on ungreased cookie sheets. Flatten balls slightly and do not refrigerate before baking. Bake as directed above.

Makes about 4½ dozen cookies

Say *Merry Christmas* in Many Ways!

Kung His Hsin Nien bing Chu Shen Tan
—CHINESE, MANDARIN

Glædelig Jul
—DANISH

Mitho Makosi Kesikansi
—CREE

Joyeux Noël
—FRENCH

Nadolig Llawen
—WELSH

Nollaig Shona Dhuit
—GAELIC (IRISH)

Kala Christouyenna!
—GREEK

Buon Natale
—ITALIAN

Boldog Karácsonyt
—HUNGARIAN

Shub Naya Baras
—HINDI

God Jul
—SWEDISH

Feliz Navidad
—SPANISH

Pozdrevlyayu s prazdnikom Rozhdestva i s Novim Godom
—RUSSIAN

Sung Tan Chuk Ha
—KOREAN

Fröhliche Weihnachten
—GERMAN

Geseënde Kersfees
—AFRIKAANS

Hyvää Joulua
—FINNISH

Mele Kalikimaka
—HAWAIIAN

Kurisumasu omedeto
—JAPANESE

Wesolych Swiat Bozego Narodzenia
—POLISH

Suksun Wan Christmas
—THAI

Light the Yule Log

Add Christmas cheer to your mantel this holiday, along with the convenience of not having to look for the matches! This small decorative touch will bring lots of warmth to your family.

WHAT YOU'LL NEED

Paper towels
Empty snack food cylinder
10×12 inches corrugated cardboard
Scissors
Hot glue gun, glue sticks
Copper spray paint
1 yard green ribbon, 2½ inches wide
Assorted Christmas greens, cut into pieces
Copper berry spray, cut into pieces
Wire cutters
Copper blossoms
Matchbox and fireplace matches

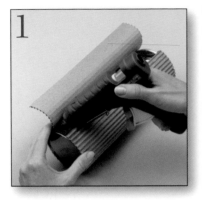

1 Use paper towels to clean inside of cylinder. Wrap corrugated cardboard around outside of cylinder. Cardboard can extend above lip of cylinder but should be flush with bottom. Trim cardboard if needed, and hot glue in place.

2 In a well-ventilated area, lightly spray cardboard with copper paint. Let dry, and repeat.

3 Tie ribbon around center of cylinder, leaving 3½-inch tails. Glue knot of ribbon to cardboard. Trim ends of ribbon into Vs.

4 Use photo as a guide to glue lengths of greens to center of knotted ribbon. Glue berry sprays to greens, then glue on blossoms.

5 Cut striking surface from matchbox, and trim as needed to fit bottom of cylinder. Glue in place on bottom of cylinder. Place matches inside cylinder.

Favorite Holiday Treats

Candy canes

Gingerbread

Chestnuts

Fruitcake

Bûche de Noël or Yule log cake

Rum balls

Chocolate truffles

Meringue kisses

Divinity

Mince pie

Pumpkin pie

Homemade fudge

Frosted sugar cookies

Toffee

Round the table

Peace and joy prevail.

May all who share this season's delight enjoy countless more.

—Chinese Blessing

Everywhere—everywhere,
Christmas tonight!
Christmas in lands of the
Fir tree and Pine,
Christmas in lands of the
Palm tree and Vine,
Christmas where snow peaks
stand solemn and white,
Christmas where cornfields
stand sunny and bright.
Christmas where peace, like
a dove in its flight
Broods o'er brave men in the
thick of the fight;
Everywhere, everywhere,
Christmas tonight!

—PHILLIPS BROOKS

CHAPTER SIX

Hark!
the Herald
Angels Sing

Hark! the herald angels sing,

Glory to the newborn King,

Peace on earth,

and mercy mild,

God and sinners reconciled.

—CHARLES WESLEY

Charles Wesley, one of the founders of Methodism, wrote thousands of hymns, including *"Hark! the Herald Angels Sing."* When he first penned the tune in 1739, it began, "Hark how all the welkin [heaven] rings/Glory to the King of Kings." Later, over Wesley's protests, a colleague altered the song to its more familiar lyrics. After Wesley's death, English musician William Cummings set the lyrics to the music we know today, which he took from a cantata written by Felix Mendelssohn in tribute to Johannes Gutenberg, the famous printer of the Bible.

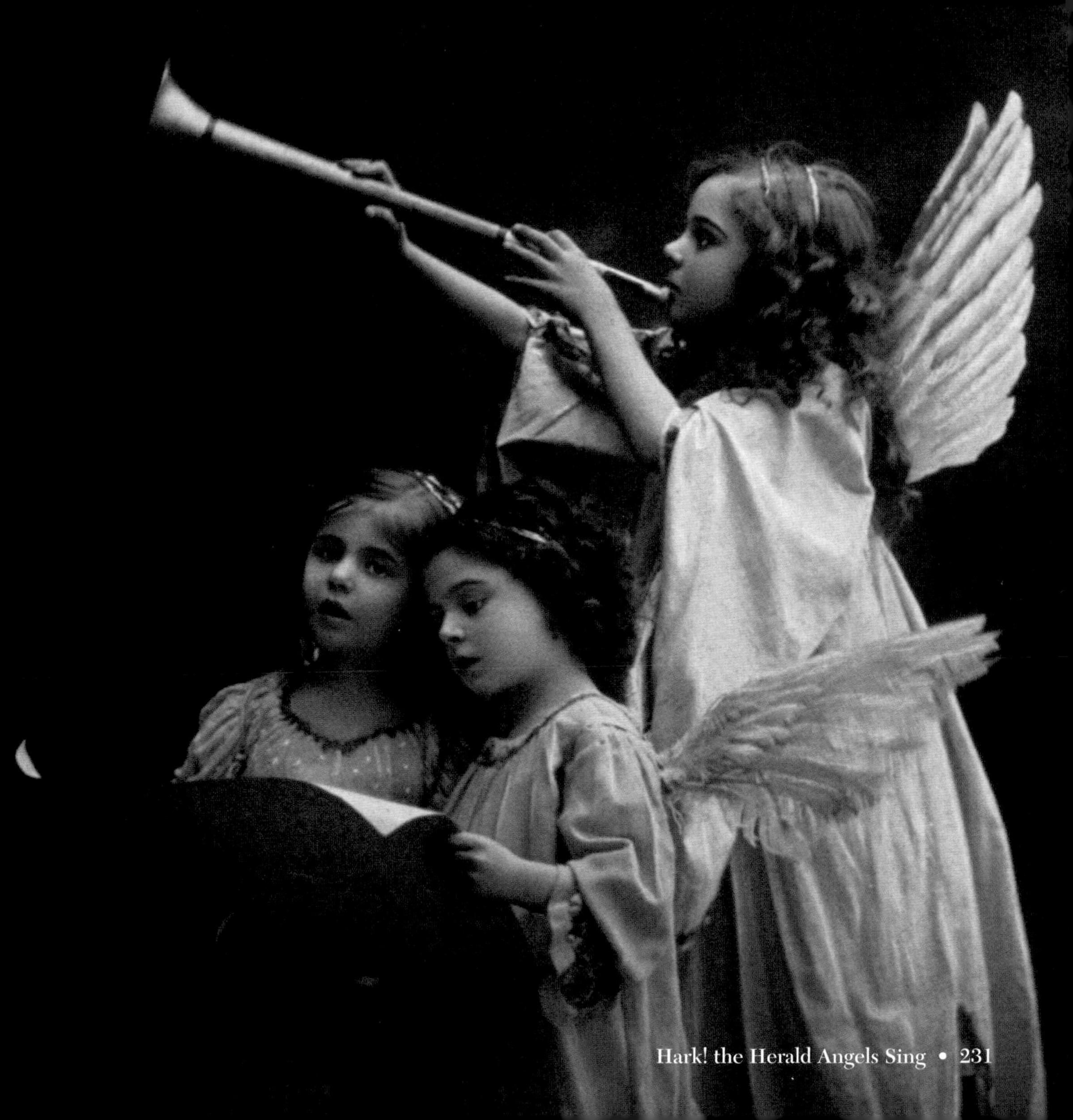

The Origins of Holiday Carols

- In 1847, the music for "O Holy Night" was written by French composer Adolphe-Charles Adam, who also wrote the ballet *Giselle*. Now a mainstay for church celebrations and carolers, the song was first denounced by church authorities for its "lack of musical taste and total absence of the spirit of religion." The English words to the song were translated from French by American clergyman John Sullivan Dwight.

- In 1857, James Pierpont, musical director at his brother's Unitarian church, was inspired to write a song about the rollicking sleigh races he watched as a young man. "Jingle Bells" was first published as "One Horse Open Sleigh," and though it was well liked from the beginning, it really took off when the Hayden Quartet recorded it in 1902.

- Pastor Phillips Brooks wrote the words to "O Little Town of Bethlehem" in 1867, recalling the view of Bethlehem from the hills of Palestine at night. His church organist, Lewis Redner, added the music so that the children's choir could sing the song.

- The song "Jolly Old St. Nicholas" is usually considered anonymous, but some people claim that it was written by Wilf Carter, also known as country singer Montana Slim.

The earth has
    grown old with its
    burden of care,
But at Christmas it
    always is young,
The heart of the
    jewel burns lustrous
    and fair
And its soul full of
    music breaks the air,
When the song of
    angels is sung.

—PHILLIPS BROOKS

I heard the bells on Christmas Day

Their old familiar

carols play,

And wild and sweet

the words repeat

Of peace on earth,

good-will to men!

—HENRY WADSWORTH
LONGFELLOW,
CHRISTMAS BELLS

Biggest Selling Christmas Song

According to the *Guinness Book of World Records,* "White Christmas" has sold more than 100 million copies around the world. The song was written by Irving Berlin and recorded by Bing Crosby for the 1942 musical *Holiday Inn.* The song appeared again in the 1954 film *White Christmas,* which starred Crosby. According to the American Society of Composers, Authors, and Publishers (ASCAP), there are more than 500 versions of "White Christmas" in dozens of languages, making it the most recorded holiday song. Released annually since 1942, the song's last chart appearance was in 1998, when it reached number 29 in the United Kingdom.

Jolly Jingle Bell Candleholder

Bring the spirit of holiday music into your home with this festive candleholder. Group a few together to create a wonderful centerpiece, or give one as a gift to your favorite holiday host.

WHAT YOU'LL NEED

9-inch-tall clear glass cylindrical vase with 3¼-inch opening

2×2-inch foam block

Low-temperature glue gun, glue sticks

8 evergreen sprigs, 6 inches each

Wire cutters

Scissors

3 sheet music pages

1 yard gold metallic ribbon, 1¾ inches wide

Ruler

Floral wire

2 red berry sprays, 12 inches each

6 holly leaves

48 gold bells, assorted sizes

Clear glass votive holder

Red votive candle

1 Glue foam block to outside bottom of vase. Insert and glue 2 evergreen sprigs horizontally at base of foam, one on each side of block. Cut remaining evergreen sprigs into short lengths, and fill in around already inserted evergreens.

2 Cut pages of sheet music in half horizontally. Tightly roll each section, and glue edges to secure. Insert and glue rolled pages into evergreens.

3 Make a 2-loop bow, with 3½-inch loops and 6-inch tails. Secure middle of bow with floral wire. V-cut ribbon ends of bow and remaining ribbon. Glue bow to front of design and remaining ribbon so that it trails out back of design.

4 Cut 1 red berry spray in half, and insert a length vertically behind bow. Insert other section beneath bow. Cut other berry spray into short lengths, and insert them around bow. Glue holly leaves into design around bow and music. Glue bell to middle of bow; add more bells as desired.

5 Fill vase with assorted bells to about 3 inches from top. Place votive holder on top of bells, and insert candle into votive.

Everybody's Doing the Jingle Bell Rock

Originally released in 1957, "Jingle Bell Rock" has been a favorite of recording artists for nearly 50 years. Who has recorded this tune?

1957 Bobby Helms

1961 Chet Atkins

1961 Eddy Arnold

1961 Bobby Rydell and Chubby Checker

1962 Bobby Vee

1963 The Platters

1964 Brenda Lee

1968 Herb Alpert

1969 Johnny Mathis

1970 Bobby Sherman

1971 Lynn Anderson

1984 Elmo & Patsy

1990 Wild Rose

1992 Neil Diamond

1992 Glen Campbell

1993 Vince Gill

1994 John Anderson

1995 Dion

1996 Flash Cadillac

1999 George Strait

1999 Amy Grant

2000 Billy Gilman

2000 Ricky Van Shelton

2003 Hilary Duff

Holidays at Rockefeller Center

In New York, it's not officially Christmastime until the tree is lit at Rockefeller Center. The first tree appeared in 1931, during the Great Depression, when workers placed a tree in the dirt of a construction site. That year, the tree symbolized Christmas as much as it did hope and the invincible human spirit. In 1933, the current tradition began with a tree decorated with 700 lights placed in front of the newly completed RCA Building. The Rockefeller Plaza Outdoor Ice-Skating Pond opened in 1936.

The decorating themes and festivities have varied from year to year. In 1941, two reindeer borrowed from the Bronx Zoo were housed in cages beside the Prometheus Fountain. In 1942, during World War II, three living trees graced the Center. In an act of patriotism, one tree was decorated in red, another in white, and the other in blue. However, because of wartime restrictions on electricity, the trees were not illuminated. In 1949, the tree was painted silver. In 1951, the entire nation witnessed the tree-lighting ceremony when it was televised on *The Kate Smith Show*. And by 1964, the ceremony had become an annual event, with celebrities such as Johnny Carson, Hugh Downs, Ed McMahon, Barbara Walters, Debbie Reynolds, Marlo Thomas, and Phil Donahue hosting the show. Today, the annual Christmas tree at Rockefeller Center is typically adorned with more than 25,000 lights but no other ornaments except for the star on top.

The Christmas tree chosen to decorate Rockefeller Center does not come from any particular forest or tree farm. Each year the manager of Rockefeller Center Gardens travels across the Northeast and elsewhere in the country searching for the perfect tree. Typically, the Christmas tree at Rockefeller Center is a Norway spruce ranging from 65 to 125 feet high and at least 35 feet wide. Since 1971, the tree has been recycled after the holidays, providing nearly 3 tons of mulch each year to the Boy Scouts of America for use at their camps.

Rankin-Bass Goes Down in History

Rudolph, Frosty, and Kris Kringle were all brought to life on television, thanks to the work of Rankin-Bass. The television production company founded by Arthur Rankin, Jr., and Jules Bass achieved fame in 1964 when they created an animated adaptation of the song "Rudolph the Red-Nosed Reindeer." Narrated by Burl Ives, with an original orchestral score by Johnny Marks, *Rudolph the Red-Nosed Reindeer* was an instant hit and today is one of the longest-running Christmas specials in television history.

Rudolph's success was soon followed by several other holiday hits produced by Rankin-Bass:

- *The Little Drummer Boy*, 1968, narrated by Greer Garson, featured the Vienna Boys' Choir
- *Frosty the Snowman*, 1969, narrated by Jimmy Durante, with Jackie Vernon as Frosty
- *Santa Claus Is Comin' to Town*, 1970, narrated by Fred Astaire, with Mickey Rooney as Kris Kringle
- *Frosty's Winter Wonderland*, 1976, narrated by Andy Griffith and starred Shelley Winters as Crystal
- *Rudolph's Shiny New Year*, 1976, with Red Skelton as Father Time
- *Nestor, the Long-Eared Christmas Donkey*, 1977, featured original music by Gene Autry
- *Jack Frost*, 1979, with songs written by Al Jolsen and Mel Tormé

Rankin-Bass trivia

- Though all of the later merchandise from *Rudolph the Red-Nosed Reindeer* features "Herbie," the elf-turned-dentist, his actual name is "Hermey."

- In the 1970s, Rankin-Bass created animated versions of *The Jackson Five Show* and *The Osmonds*.

- Rankin-Bass television specials were produced using stop-motion animation. This early type of technology gives the appearance that still objects are moving. The object is photographed in a single frame, then moved ever so slightly before being photographed again. When the frames are put together, the objects appear to move by themselves. Stop-motion animation is similar to a cartoon but is produced with real objects instead of drawings.

Notes on the Nutcracker

In 1890, following the success of the Russian ballets *Swan Lake* and *Sleeping Beauty*, composer Peter Tchaikovsky, choreographers Marius Petipa and Lev Ivanov, and set designer Ivan Vsevolozhsky created what would become one of the best-loved ballets of all time. *The Nutcracker*, a full-length ballet, was based on *The Nutcracker of Nuremberg*, by

Alexandre Dumas, which he adapted from *The Nutcracker and the Mouse King*, by German writer E.T.A. Hoffman. In December 1892, the ballet opened at the Mariinsky Theatre of Russia to mixed reviews. It wasn't until 1944 that an American ballet company performed the masterpiece. Choreographed by W. Christensen, the San Francisco Opera Ballet produced the first full-length American production, with Jocelyn Vollmar dancing as the Snow Queen.

Caroling

Nothing warms the heart quite like Christmas caroling. The holidays can be hectic, and the spirit of Christmas can easily become lost in the rush and worry of getting everything "just right." Last year on the day before Christmas Eve, eight of us decided to take a much-needed break and spend the evening caroling with our children. Setting out with the intention of lifting the spirits of our neighbors, we spread Christmas cheer until we were tired, chilled, and admittedly, grouchy.

One more house, we decided, and piling into our cars again we spotted the perfect target. The lonely-looking elderly man sitting in his kitchen window seemed like he needed us. Pulling over, we parked our cars in front of his house and argued about which songs to sing. Half of the children were either whining or crying about the cold, and the beautiful Utah snow seemed to have lost its sparkle despite our good intentions.

We finally settled on four songs for the man, then rang the bell and waited for him to open his door. Already thinking about getting the kids to bed and the work I had yet to do, I automatically started in on "We Wish You a Merry Christmas" with the others. But as the man stood in the doorway, his eyes filling with tears, my sidetracked thoughts came to a screeching halt. As we sang, I could hear the emotion in many of my friends' voices, and my singing grew softer as I fought the tears myself.

The elderly gentleman stood in his doorway, the kitchen light behind him lighting his soft silver hair like a gentle halo. He clapped with delight

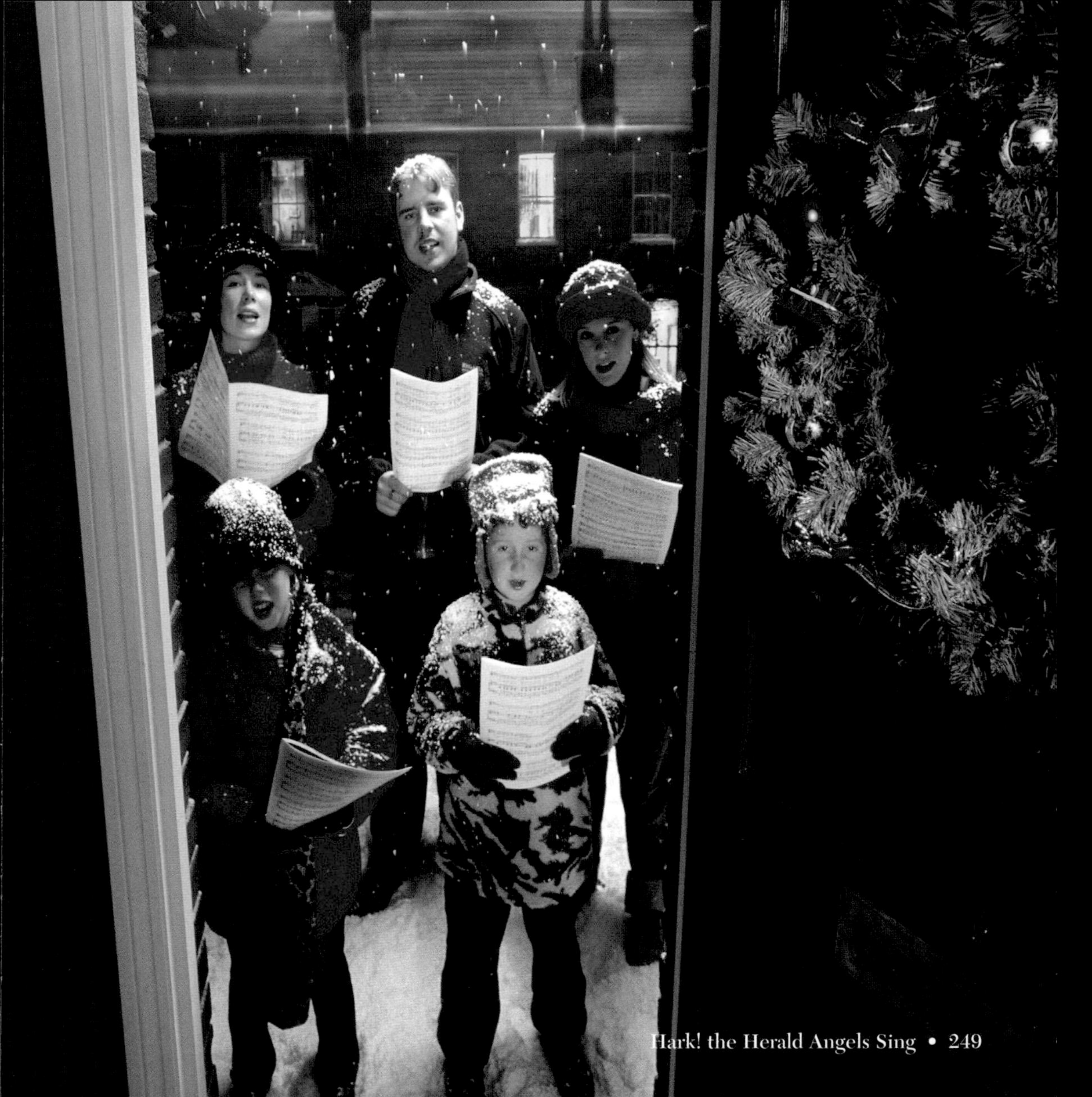

one had greeted us with such joy and enthusiasm all night. No one had made us feel so welcomed and so loved. Finishing up with "Silent Night," we sang as sweetly and lovingly as we could, and his own shaky voice joined in with us. Tears streamed down my cold cheeks.

Thanking us profusely and wishing us a merry Christmas, he happily went back inside his warm home. We slowly and regrettably left the man, whose spirit and tears made all the difference in our night, indeed, all the difference in our Christmas. Although he had sat alone in his window, looking as if he needed us, we had no idea how much we needed him.

—SUSAN FAHNCKE

as we finished the first song and glided right into the next. Warm air emptied out of his front door, but he didn't seem to care: He was so happy with our visit. He seemed to personify the spirit of Christmas, and I felt a guilty twinge about my grouchiness.

True joy began to fill my soul as I sang my heart out for this man. No

Largest Caroling Service

The world's largest caroling service took place December 20, 2003, as recorded by the *Guinness Book of World Records.* Organized by the City of Cambridge in Ontario, Canada, 1,175 carolers sang Christmas songs in the Civic Square for 28 minutes.

The Vienna Boys' Choir

Giving voice to the holidays, the Vienna Boys' Choir is one of the oldest boys' choirs in the world. According to founding documents, the choir has roots as far back as 1498, when Maximilian I brought a dozen boys together to form the court music band.

As expected, the choir has produced many musicians that shaped the musical history of the 19th and 20th centuries, including composers Joseph and Michael Haydn. Franz Schubert wrote his first compositions as a court choirboy, and although he was considered a musical genius, he was not a favorite of his teachers since he was more interested in writing music than in getting good grades for his schoolwork.

In 1924, the choir began singing in concert halls around the world. Since then, the Vienna Boys' Choir has performed concerts under many great conductors, including Leonard Bernstein. Yet, in keeping with a tradition dating back to 1498, the choir sings solemn mass in Vienna's Hofburg Chapel every Sunday.

Mulled Apple Cider

2 quarts bottled apple cider or juice (not unfiltered)

¼ cup packed light brown sugar

1 square (8 inches) double-thickness cheesecloth

8 allspice berries

4 cinnamon sticks, broken into halves

Cotton string

12 whole cloves

1 large orange

Additional cinnamon sticks (optional)

1. Combine apple cider and brown sugar in slow cooker. Rinse cheesecloth. Wrap allspice berries and cinnamon stick halves in cheesecloth; tie securely with cotton string. Stick cloves randomly into orange; cut into quarters. Place spice bag and orange quarters in cider mixture.

2. Cover; cook on HIGH 2½ to 3 hours.

3. Once cooked, cider may be turned to LOW and kept warm up to 3 additional hours. Remove spice bag and orange before serving. Ladle cider into mugs. Garnish with additional cinnamon sticks, if desired.

Makes 10 servings

RADIO CITY MUSIC HALL
Christmas Spectacular

Since 1933, the Radio City Music Hall *Christmas Spectacular* has been a mainstay for the holidays in New York City. Originally performed before movie screenings, the *Christmas Spectacular* expanded to its current 90-minute live stage production in 1979. For eight weeks each year, the show attracts more than a million people to its Big Apple performances, and thousands more catch its holiday tour to major cities around the United States. It is the number one live show in the country. Part of the allure of the show is its over-the-top presentation:

- The cast changes costumes eight times during the show, with as little as 78 seconds to do so. In all, there are 1,300 costumes worn.
- During the "Music Hall Menagerie," two donkeys, three camels, five sheep, and a horse make a special appearance. They have their own staff of trainers offstage.
- A real ice rink built on a movable platform is used during the "Christmas in New York" scene.
- The "Here Comes Santa Claus" number features every member of the cast dressed as Santa to explain how Santa can actually deliver gifts to every boy and girl in the world, all in one night.
- During the show's run, 2,500 pounds of "snow" fall upon the stage.

TOP 20
Christmas Songs

According to ASCAP, these are the most-performed holiday songs from 2000 to 2005

1. **The Christmas Song** (Chestnuts Roasting on an Open Fire) (MEL TORMÉ, ROBERT WELLS)

2. **Santa Claus Is Coming to Town** (J. FRED COOTS, HAVEN GILLESPIE)

3. **Have Yourself a Merry Little Christmas** (RALPH BLANE, HUGH MARTIN)

4. **Winter Wonderland** (FELIX BERNARD, RICHARD B. SMITH)

5. **White Christmas** (IRVING BERLIN)

6. **Let It Snow! Let It Snow! Let It Snow!** (SAMMY CAHN, JULE STYNE)

7. **Rudolph the Red-Nosed Reindeer** (JOHNNY MARKS)

8. **Jingle Bell Rock** (JOSEPH CARLETON BEAL, JAMES ROSS BOOTHE)

9. **I'll Be Home for Christmas** (WALTER KENT, KIM GANNON, BUCK RAM)

10. **Little Drummer Boy** (KATHERINE K. DAVIS, HENRY V. ONORATI, HARRY SIMEONE)

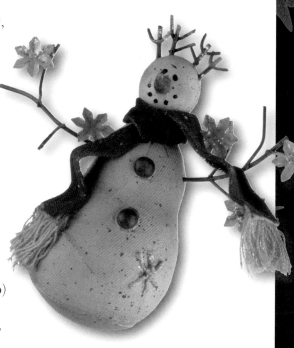

11. **Sleigh Ride** (Leroy Anderson, Mitchell Parish)

12. **It's the Most Wonderful Time of the Year** (Edward Pola, George Wyle)

13. **Silver Bells** (Jay Livingston, Ray Evans)

14. **Rockin' Around the Christmas Tree** (Johnny Marks)

15. **Feliz Navidad** (José Feliciano)

16. **Blue Christmas** (Billy Hayes, Jay W. Johnson)

17. **Frosty the Snowman** (Steve Nelson, Walter E. Rollins)

18. **A Holly Jolly Christmas** (Johnny Marks)

19. **I Saw Mommy Kissing Santa Claus** (Tommie Connor)

20. **Here Comes Santa Claus** (Gene Autry, Oakley Haldeman)

Jingle Bells

JAMES PIERPONT

Dashing through the snow

In a one-horse open sleigh;

O'er the fields we go,

Laughing all the way.

Bells on bobtail ring,

Making spirits bright,

What fun it is to ride and sing a sleighing song tonight!

Jingle bells! Jingle bells! Jingle all the way!

Oh, what fun it is to ride

In a one-horse open sleigh.

So here comes Gabriel again, and what he says is, "Good tidings of great joy… for all people." …That's why the shepherds are first: They represent all the nameless, all the working stiffs, the great wheeling population of the whole world.

—WALTER WANGERIN, JR.,
PREPARING FOR JESUS

christmas quiz

In a scene from the 1983 movie A Christmas Story, *Ralphie tells Santa what he wants for Christmas.*

1. What is the title to the song that begins, "Chestnuts roasting on an open fire..."?

2. How many reindeer does Santa have?

3. What Christmas tune was first published as a lullaby?

4. What were Frosty the Snowman's last words?

5. Who played George Bailey in *It's a Wonderful Life*?

6. What danced in the children's heads in *'Twas the Night Before Christmas*?

7. Which reindeer isn't mentioned in *'Twas the Night Before Christmas*?

8. In *A Christmas Story*, what toy did Ralphie want more than anything?

Answers: 1. "The Christmas Song"; 2. eight (nine, including Rudolph); 3. "Away in a Manger"; 4. "I'll be back again someday"; 5. Jimmy Stewart; 6. visions of sugarplums; 7. Rudolph; 8. Red Ryder BB Gun

The merry family gatherings—
The old, the very young;
The strangely lovely way they
Harmonize in carols sung.
For Christmas is tradition time—
Traditions that recall
The precious memories down the years,
The sameness of them all.

—HELEN LOWRIE MARSHALL

Let's dance and sing and make good cheer, For Christmas comes but once a year.

—SIR GEORGE ALEXANDER MACFARREN, *FROM A FRAGMENT*

Santa Claus Is Coming to Town

Oh! You better watch out,

You better not cry,

You better not pout,

I'm telling you why:

Santa Claus is
coming to town!

—J. FRED COOTS AND HAVEN GILLESPIE

When musician J. Fred Coots and lyricist Haven Gillespie first composed *"Santa Claus Is Coming to Town"* in 1932, it took two years to convince someone to perform their song. Considered a "kiddie song," it didn't become a hit until the wife of entertainer Eddie Cantor coaxed her husband into performing the song on his radio show. Later, Perry Como, and Bing Crosby with the Andrews Sisters had multimillion-selling recordings of the song, making it one of the most popular Christmas carols of all time. The success of the song inspired a Rankin-Bass animated production in 1970, which was narrated by Fred Astaire, with Mickey Rooney as the voice of Kris Kringle.

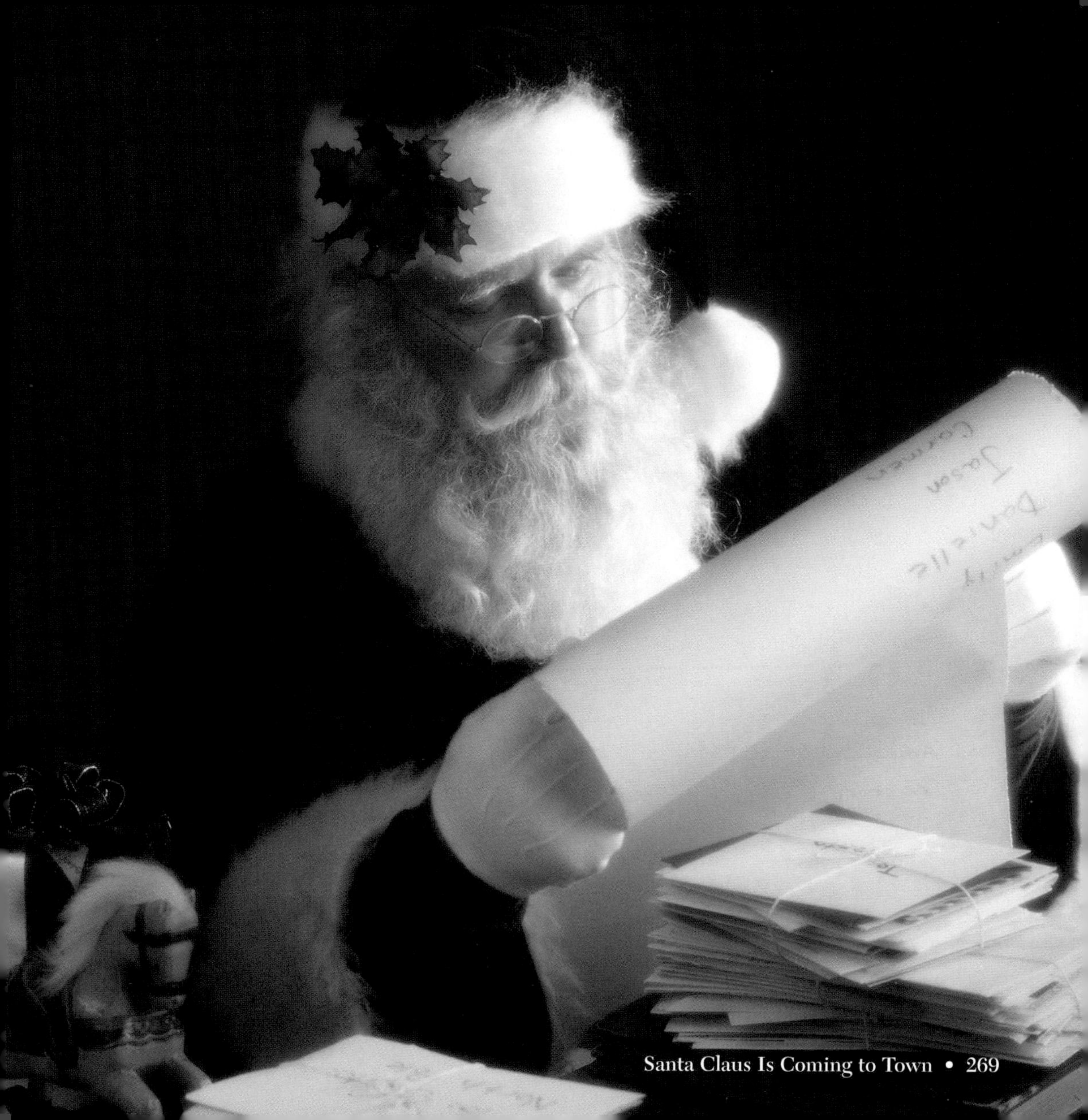
Carmen
Jason
Danielle

Who Is Santa Claus?

For centuries, St. Nicholas has been remembered by Christians for his generosity toward children and the poor. The real St. Nicholas lived in Turkey, where he served as bishop in the town of Myra, during the fourth century. According to Dutch legend, *Sinter Klaas* (St. Nicholas) brought gifts at Christmastime, either through an open window or down a chimney. This legend is the basis of the Santa Claus we know and love today.

Prior to the 16th century, gifts were exchanged during the feast of St. Nicholas on December 6. After that time, German Protestants began celebrating *Christkindl* on December 25, a feast day for the Christ Child. Soon the two days merged into one, although, today many people in Europe continue to celebrate both days.

As early as 1773, the name "St. A Claus" appeared in print. But Americans did not have a detailed description of St. Nicholas until Washington Irving included a drawing of him in the 1809 publication *A History of New York*. Then, in 1823, Clement Clarke Moore wrote *'Twas the Night Before Christmas* (or *A Visit from St. Nicholas*). It was Moore's account that characterized Santa as a jolly old man who rides in a sleigh pulled by flying reindeer and slides down chimneys to deliver gifts.

A merry CHRISTMAS

Yes, Virginia, There Is a Santa Claus

In 1897, eight-year-old Virginia O'Hanlon asked the question, "Is there a Santa Claus?" She wrote a letter to the editor of *The New York Sun* requesting an honest reply. This is what her letter said:

> Dear Editor:
> I am eight years old. Some of my little friends say there is no Santa Claus. Papa says, "If you see it in *The Sun,* it's so." Please tell me the truth, is there a Santa Claus?
>
> Virginia O'Hanlon
> 115 West Ninety-Fifth Street

An editor for *The Sun,* Francis P. Church, received Virginia's letter and wrote the following reply. It was printed in the September 21, 1897, edition of *The New York Sun.*

Virginia,

    Your little friends are wrong. They have been affected by the skepticism of a skeptical age. They do not believe except [what] they see. They think that nothing can be which is not comprehensible by their little minds. All minds, Virginia, whether they be men's or children's, are little. In this great universe of ours, man is a mere insect, an ant, in his intellect, as compared with the boundless world about him, as measured by the intelligence capable of grasping the whole of truth and knowledge.

Yes, Virginia, there is a Santa Claus. He exists as certainly as love and generosity and devotion exist, and you know that they abound and give to your life its highest beauty and joy. Alas! how dreary would be the world if there were no Santa Claus. It would be as dreary as if there were no Virginias. There would be no child-like faith then, no poetry, no romance to make tolerable this existence. We should have no enjoyment, except in sense and sight. The eternal light with which childhood fills the world would be extinguished.

Not believe in Santa Claus! You might as well not believe in fairies! You might get your papa to hire men to watch in all the chimneys on Christmas Eve to catch Santa Claus, but even if they did not see Santa Claus coming down, what would that prove? Nobody sees Santa Claus, but that is no sign that there is no Santa Claus. The most real things in the world are those that neither children nor men can see. Did you ever see fairies dancing on the lawn? Of course not, but that's no proof that they are not there.

Nobody can conceive or imagine all the wonders there are unseen and unseeable in the world.

You may tear apart the baby's rattle and see what makes the noise inside, but there is a veil covering the unseen world which not the strongest man, nor even the united strength of all the strongest men that ever lived, could tear apart. Only faith, fancy, poetry, love, romance, can push aside that curtain and view and picture the supernal beauty and glory beyond. Is it all real? Ah, Virginia, in all this world there is nothing else real and abiding.

No Santa Claus! Thank God! He lives, and he lives forever. A thousand years from now, Virginia, nay, ten times ten thousand years from now, he will continue to make glad the heart of childhood.

Looking for Santa Claus? Try these U.S. towns: Santa Claus, Indiana, with a population of approximately 2,200, and Santa Claus, Georgia, with about 240 residents. Or you might try North Pole, Alaska, but rumor has it that *he actually lives in Finland.*

I don't know, Santa,

you're just furrier

than I expected.

—ANONYMOUS

Linzer Sandwich Cookies

1⅓ cups all-purpose flour
¼ teaspoon baking powder
¼ teaspoon salt
¾ cup granulated sugar
½ cup (1 stick) butter, softened
1 egg
1 teaspoon vanilla
    Powdered sugar (optional)
    Seedless red raspberry jam

1. Place flour, baking powder, and salt in small bowl; stir. Beat granulated sugar and butter in medium bowl with electric mixer at medium speed until light and fluffy. Beat in egg and vanilla. Gradually add flour mixture. Beat at low speed until dough forms. Divide dough in half; wrap each half in plastic wrap and refrigerate 2 hours or until firm.

2. Preheat oven to 375°F. Working with one portion at a time, roll dough on lightly floured surface to ³⁄₁₆-inch thickness. Cut dough into desired shapes with floured cookie cutters. Cut even numbers of each shape. (If dough becomes too soft, refrigerate several minutes before continuing.) Cut 1-inch centers out of half the cutouts of each shape. Reroll trimmings and cut more shapes. Place cutouts 2 inches apart on ungreased cookie sheets. Bake 7 to 9 minutes or until edges are lightly brown. Let cookies stand on cookie sheets 1 to 2 minutes. Remove cookies to wire racks; cool completely.

3. Sprinkle cookies with holes with powdered sugar, if desired. Spread jam on flat sides of whole cookies, spreading almost to edges. Place cookies with holes, flat sides down, over jam. Store tightly covered at room temperature or freeze up to 3 months.

Makes about 2 dozen cookies

My idea of Christmas,

whether old-fashioned or modern, is very simple:

loving others. Come to think of it,

why do we have to wait for Christmas to do that?

—Bob Hope

He who has not Christmas

in his heart will never find it under a tree.

—Roy L. Smith

Tracking Santa Claus

"Deter. Detect. Defend." This motto of the North American Aerospace Defense Command, better known as NORAD, applies to the Canadian and American agency's responsibility to defend the airspace of Canada, Alaska, and the continental United States. However, each December 24, NORAD is also involved in tracking Santa Claus's sleigh ride across the globe.

Using data obtained from a worldwide network of radar and satellites in space, NORAD staff and more than 360 volunteers begin reporting on Santa's progress at 5:00 A.M. MST. Real-time updates via e-mail, the Internet, and telecasts are transferred into streaming audio and video updates and then translated into French, Japanese, Spanish, Portuguese, and English.

Which Cities Are Easiest for Santa to Visit?

Those with snow, of course! According to the Statistical Abstract of the United States, the average snowfall each December in the following locations is more than two feet:

- Valdez, Alaska
- Yakutat, Alaska
- Blue Canyon, California
- Marquette, Michigan
- Muskegon, Michigan
- Sault Sainte Marie, Michigan
- Mount Washington, New Hampshire
- Syracuse, New York

He Does Exist!

Yes, Santa Claus really does exist—and he lives in Rovaniemi, Finland! At Santa's Village, you can visit Santa in his workshop and watch his trusty elves building toys and decorating for the holidays. You can also stop by one of the gift shops and pick up Santa's favorite Finnish candies or a toy from Santa's workshop.

In keeping with Santa's North Pole address, Santa's Village is located in the Finnish Lapland on the Arctic Circle. The Lapland is a region that includes northern Finland, Sweden, and Norway. It is north of the Arctic Circle, an imaginary line on the surface of the earth where the sun does not rise on the winter solstice or set on the summer solstice.

Santa's Favorite Reads

Which stories does Santa curl up with on a cold winter's night?

Olive, the Other Reindeer,
J. Otto Seibold and Vivian Walsh

How the Grinch Stole Christmas, Dr. Seuss

Saint Francis and the Christmas Donkey, Robert Byrd

The Polar Express, Chris Van Allsburg

Christmas in the Big House, Christmas in the Quarters, Patricia C. McKissack and Fredrick L. McKissack

"The Gift of the Magi," O. Henry

The Snowman, Raymond Briggs

The Wild Christmas Reindeer, Jan Brett

'Twas the Night Before Christmas

CLEMENT CLARKE MOORE

'Twas the night before Christmas, and all through the house,
Not a creature was stirring, not even a mouse.
The stockings were hung by the chimney with care,
In the hope that St. Nicholas soon would be there.

The children were nestled all snug in their beds,
While visions of sugarplums danced in their heads.
And Mama in her kerchief, and I in my cap,
Had just settled our brains for a long winter's nap,

When out on the lawn there arose such a clatter,
I sprang from my bed to see what was the matter.
Away to the window I flew like a flash,
Tore open the shutters and threw up the sash.

The moon on the breast of the new-fallen snow
Gave the luster of midday to objects below.
When what to my wondering eyes should appear
But a miniature sleigh and eight tiny reindeer.

With a little old driver, so lively and quick,
I knew in a moment it must be St. Nick!
More rapid than eagles his coursers they came,
And he whistled and shouted and called them by name:

"Now, Dasher! Now, Dancer! Now, Prancer! Now, Vixen!
On, Comet! On, Cupid! On, Donner and Blitzen!
To the top of the porch! To the top of the wall!
Now, dash away! Dash away! Dash away, all!"

As dry leaves that before the wild hurricane fly,
When they meet with an obstacle, mount to the sky,
So up to the housetop the coursers they flew,
With a sleigh full of toys, and St. Nicholas, too.

And then in a twinkling I heard on the roof
The prancing and pawing of each tiny hoof.
As I drew in my head and was turning around,
Down the chimney St. Nicholas came with a bound.

He was dressed all in fur from his head to his foot,
And his clothes were all tarnished with ashes and soot;
A bundle of toys he had flung on his back,
And he looked like a peddler just opening his pack.

His eyes, how they twinkled! His dimples, how merry!
His cheeks were like roses, his nose like a cherry;
His droll little mouth was drawn up like a bow,
And the beard on his chin was as white as the snow.

The stump of a pipe he held tight in his teeth,
And the smoke, it encircled his head like a wreath.
He had a broad face and a little round belly
That shook when he laughed, like a bowl full of jelly.

He was chubby and plump, a right jolly old elf,
And I laughed when I saw him, in spite of myself.
A wink of his eye and a twist of his head,
Soon gave me to know I had nothing to dread.

He spoke not a word, but went straight to his work,
And filled all the stockings, then turned with a jerk.
And laying a finger aside of his nose,
And giving a nod, up the chimney he rose.

He sprang to his sleigh, to his team gave a whistle,
And away they all flew like the down of a thistle.
But I heard him exclaim, ere he drove out of sight,
"Merry Christmas to all, and to all a good night!"

Rum Fruitcake Cookies

1 cup sugar

¾ cup shortening

3 eggs

⅓ cup orange juice

1 tablespoon rum extract

3 cups all-purpose flour

2 teaspoons baking powder

1 teaspoon baking soda

1 teaspoon salt

2 cups (8 ounces) chopped candied mixed fruit

1 cup raisins

1 cup nuts, coarsely chopped

1. Preheat oven to 375°F. Lightly grease cookie sheets; set aside. Beat sugar and shortening in large bowl until fluffy. Add eggs, orange juice, and rum extract; beat 2 minutes.

2. Combine flour, baking powder, baking soda, and salt in medium bowl. Add candied fruit, raisins, and nuts. Stir into creamed mixture. Drop dough by rounded teaspoonfuls 2 inches apart onto prepared cookie sheets.

3. Bake 10 to 12 minutes or until golden brown. Let stand on cookie sheets 2 minutes. Remove to wire racks; cool completely. *Makes about 6 dozen cookies*

Jolly Old St. Nicholas

When the clock is striking twelve,
When I'm fast asleep,
Down the chimney broad and black,
With your pack you'll creep;
All the stockings you will find
Hanging in a row;
Mine will be the shortest one,
You'll be sure to know.

—Author Unknown,
from "Jolly Old St. Nicholas"

Santa's Aliases

Christmas gifts are bestowed by different gift givers in various countries. These include Père Noël in France, St. Nicholas or Sinter Klaas in Holland, Father Christmas in England, the Three Kings in parts of Latin America and Spain, and Santa Claus in the United States. In Germany, children are visited by Christkind, an angelic messenger of

Jesus. Babouschka, a grandmotherly figure, brings presents in Russia, while in Sweden, Jultomten, a gnome who rides a sleigh, does the honors. Syrian children receive gifts from a camel of one of the Three Wise Men, reportedly the smallest one in the caravan. And in Italy, a kindly old witch named La Befana leaves gifts for children.

Look skyward, toward the Christmas moon.
Old St. Nick's expected soon!
Sleigh bells ringing 'round his sled,
It's almost time to go to bed.
Leave Santa's treat to spread good cheer,
And don't forget his eight reindeer.
Sweep the hearth to clear the soot,
Clear a path for Santa's foot.
Light a candle, point the way,
Santa Claus arrives today.

Reindeer Hooves

"Mommy, Mommy! Do you think they left the North Pole yet?" my four-year-old son anxiously queried in an unusually deep voice.

"Gosh, I don't know, Kev," I replied. But then, after thinking about the anticipation in his eyes and voice, I corrected myself and said decidedly, "Oh, yes, absolutely, positively, yes. Santa and the reindeer have definitely left the North Pole by now."

This little imp of a child grinned from ear to ear and began describing what the reindeer were discussing on their flight through the sky as they visited every child in the world. Rudolph, of course, was the brightest because he was smart enough to turn his nose on and off like a blinking red light. He would tell them what the weather was, which country they would visit first, what the dangers were of landing on a weak roof, and to listen only to Santa for their directions. He reminded me that "even the reindeers are not allowed to talk to strangers," as if there would be a lot of them racing around the sky.

Kevin began to sift through Christmas cookies to find the most perfect cookies to leave for Santa. After much debate, he decided that "this reindeer with the chocolate horns looks like the one Santa would want. So does this angel with yellow sprinkles and this toy soldier with a big red hat and this star like the one that saw Jesus . . . ."

He gently put them onto the dish he made in nursery school, licking his fingers after each placement and

picking off a chocolate sprinkle or two. Kev poured Santa a glass of milk, placed it next to the cookies on the dish, and toddled to bed as he wondered when they would arrive.

"Do you think Santa will knock or come down the chimney? Will he burn his tummy, or does he have on fireproof underwear? Can the reindeer come in, too?" Finally, the little guy with the twinkling brown eyes and mop of chestnut hair could not think of any more things to say, and he fell asleep until around midnight when I heard him shriek, "I hear them, I hear them! They're on the roof! Santa's reindeers are on the roof!" He barreled down the stairs, and as he tornadoed through the kitchen he stopped on a dime, practically falling on the cookie dish. His eyes looked as though they would pop out of his head as he breathlessly sang, "Santa ate all the cookies! Santa ate all the cookies! Look, Mommy, they're gone and the milk is gone and look, the crumbs are everywhere! I bet he fed the reindeers, too!" Kevin never did convince his brother and sister that he had heard reindeer hooves on the roof. But he believed it . . . for years and years and years. . . .

—ELIZABETH TOOLE

Holiday Points to Ponder

- What exactly are "reindeer games"?

- Why is the tree trunk on an artificial tree green instead of brown?

- Who brings Santa *his* Christmas gifts?

- Why is Rudolph's nose red?

- How does Santa deliver gifts if you don't have a chimney?

Reindeer Facts

- Reindeer are one of several subspecies of caribou found around the world.

- Reindeer are herbivores, which means they eat vegetation. In the summer, they eat leaves and herbs. In the winter, they eat lichen and moss.

- Reindeer generally don't run very fast. In fact, a white-tailed deer could outrun a reindeer.

- Reindeer use their antlers like a shovel to break through the crust of snow to reach the vegetation underneath.

- Reindeer are various colors, including white, dark gray, and brown. Males can have light-colored manes, necks, and shoulders.

Go, Girls, Go!

The only female deer to grow antlers are reindeer. Each summer, both males and females grow their wonderful racks, but males usually shed theirs in late November to mid-December. Females keep their antlers until spring. Because all of Santa's reindeer are depicted with antlers, one might conclude that every one of them, including Rudolph, is female.

Up on the Housetop

B. R. HANBY

Up on the housetop reindeer pause,
Out jumps good old Santa Claus;
Down through the chimney with lots of toys,
All for the little ones' Christmas joys.

Ho, ho, ho! Who wouldn't go!
Ho, ho, ho! Who wouldn't go!
Up on the housetop,
Click, click, click,
Down through the chimney with good St. Nick.

First comes the stocking of little Nell;
Oh, dear Santa, fill it well;
Give her a dolly that laughs and cries,
One that can open and shut its eyes.

Next comes the stocking of little Bill;
Oh, just see that glorious fill!
Here is a hammer and lots of tacks,
Whistle and ball and a set of jacks.

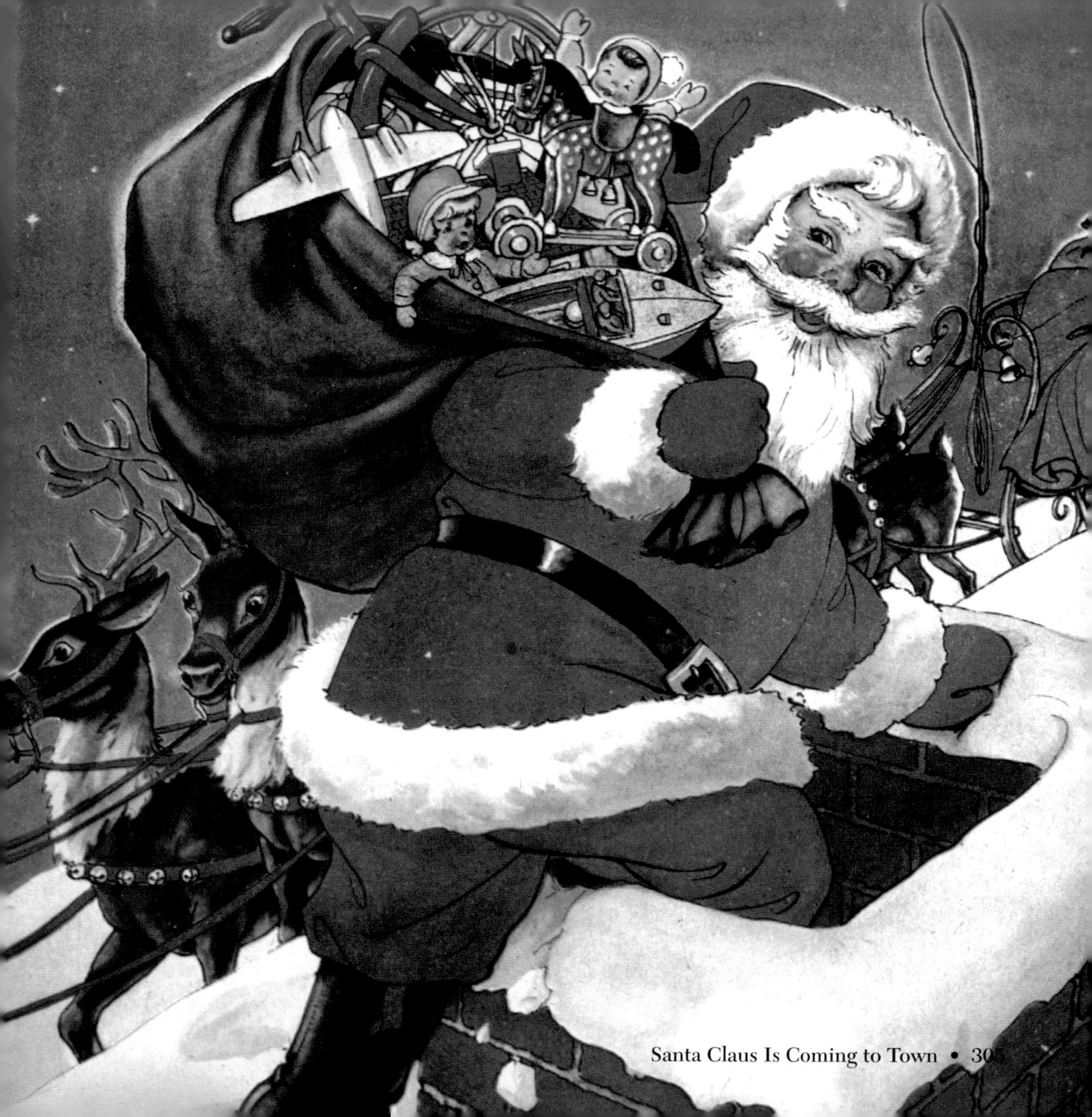

Slip, Slide, and Skate Penguin Jar

This spunky little fellow will add an element of fun to a gift container holding a holiday treat. With the pattern provided, see just how easy and quick it is to paint.

WHAT YOU'LL NEED

Pencil
Tracing paper
Ruler
Scissors
Tape
Clear glass sealable jar with 4×4-inch side surfaces
Enamel paint: white, green, yellow, red, black
#2 round paintbrushes
Bottle-tip nozzle pen set

1 Enlarge pattern on page 308 and trace onto tracing paper. Cut pattern paper to 3×3½ inches. Position and tape pattern inside glass jar.

Enlarge pattern 200%.

2 Thin a small amount of white paint with water. Hold jar level, with pattern side up. Paint inner body of penguin white, leaving beak shape clear. Thin a small amount of green enamel, and paint tree shapes. Repeat with yellow to paint beak and feet, red to fill in red hat stripes, and black to paint penguin's body. Let dry; repeat if necessary.

3 Using pen set, attach extension cap and fine metal tip to black enamel bottle. Practice squeezing enamel from bottle, then paint skate blade lines and 2 small dots for eyes. (Quickly and thoroughly rinse out cap and metal tip after each use and change of color.)

4 Attach extension cap and fine metal tip to white enamel bottle. Apply enamel thickly to achieve look of textured snow along bottom edges of trees, beneath penguin's skates, behind penguin, and around sides of jar. With white enamel, paint pompom, hatband, white hat stripes, and snowflakes around upper portion of jar.

5 Remove rubber stopper from jar and follow manufacturer's instructions on enamel bottles for drying, baking, and curing enamel to the glass.

christmas trivia

1. Which of these states has a town named Santa Claus?
    a. Vermont
    b. Colorado
    c. Maine
    d. Indiana

2. What color is Santa's belt?
    a. Green
    b. Red
    c. Black
    d. White

3. Who gave Santa the nickname Kris Kringle?
    a. Charles Dickens
    b. Martin Luther
    c. Charles Schulz
    d. Grover Cleveland

4. What do they call Santa Claus in Chile?
    a. Old Man Christmas
    b. Señor Santa
    c. Claus the Good
    d. El Claus

5. What is the rabbit's name in the holiday television special *Frosty the Snowman*?
    a. Roger
    b. Hocus Pocus
    c. Thumper
    d. Peter

Answers: 1: d; 2: c; 3: b; 4: a; 5: b

The American image of Santa Claus was brought to life by Thomas Nast's drawings of Santa Claus for *Harper's Weekly.* He presented Santa with a long white beard, sleigh, and reindeer. The January 3, 1863, issue had "Santa Claus in Camp," depicting Santa and his reindeer (upper corners), with the focal point being a lonely soldier in the U.S. Civil War separated from his wife and children.

Never worry about the size of your Christmas tree. In the eyes of children, *they are all 30 feet tall.*

—LARRY WILDE

Children building snow

people, snow falling softly,

Christmas lights twinkling—

BELIEVE

in the magic that is Christmas.

"*Merry Christmas to all,*
And to all a good night!"

—St. Nicholas,
'Twas the Night Before Christmas,
by Clement Clarke Moore

Index